THE ART CURE

THE
ART
CURE

A Memoir of Abuse and Fortune

BRIDGETTE MAYER

With a Foreword by Michael Gerber, Author of THE E-MYTH

THE ART CURE

A Memoir of Abuse and Fortune

ISBN   978-1-61961-498-7 *Paperback*

978-1-61961-499-4 *Ebook*

LIONCREST
PUBLISHING

This is for you, Mom. Your dream to have little girls in your life and your fight to adopt led me into a beautiful world. I would not be on this planet, thriving as I am, without the love and support from you and Dad. I love you both dearly.

CONTENTS

FOREWORD

By Michael Gerber

WHAT CAN A MAN AT EIGHTY SAY ABOUT A WOMAN in her forties if not, "Watch what she did, but understand it, lest you make the wrong decision?"

The Art Cure is a story of extreme independent mindedness, driven by curiosity and fear.

Fear, because the world has told you it is dangerous.

Independent mindedness, because the world has told you it is yours to shape, and only yours.

Bridgette shaped her world, and Bridgette's world shaped Bridgette.

The outcome, and the story that speaks of it, is splendidly revealed in this wonderful book.

There is nothing more compelling to me as an author, and as a man who has helped millions shape their world—and who have been shaped by it—than a great story of one who has exceeded all reasonable expectations.

Bridgette didn't have a plan.

She didn't know where she was going.

Bridgette's world revealed itself each and every step along the way, leading to that all-encompassing question: "Now What?" Again and again and again.

Bridgette's remarkably intuitive answers are a treasure trove for anyone facing that very same dilemma: "Now What?" As that's the story of every one of our lives.

"Now What?"

Read, and enjoy!

– MICHAEL GERBER, AUTHOR OF *THE E-MYTH* AND
CREATOR OF THE E-MYTH REVOLUTION

INTRODUCTION

THE LIPSTICK MURAL

The apartment I grew up in was utterly bare. There was no furniture, no toys, no food, and no joy. My siblings and I did not go to school, or have friends, and we almost never had anything to eat. There was absolutely nothing a typical little girl would play with, and I had to be resourceful in finding ways to keep my mind occupied.

One of my earliest memories of color—when I was only 4 or 5—is when I found my mother's cotton makeup bag. It was the only object of abundance in our filthy tenement. Inside, I discovered a Technicolor dreamland of brilliant pink and red lipsticks, purple- and blue-hued eye shadows, rosy blushes, creamy green eyeliners, and black goopy mascara.

The cacophony of color and texture was too enticing to resist; all my senses were awakened within that makeup bag. The powders, chalks, and oils of the various products were a delight to my little fingers and the exotic smells tickled my nose.

I felt compelled to draw, but there were no surfaces on which to apply the color, save the dirty walls that held us in. Once I started, I couldn't stop. Using the only materials available to me, I drew all over the walls. I was mesmerized by the splashes of vibrant color I had created. Inspired, I kept at it until all of the makeup was used up. I remember feeling deeply satisfied—giddy with happiness and pride—at having created something so beautiful. But I was also afraid. Instinctually, I knew my mother would not be as proud of my lipstick mural as I was, and I knew there would be hell to pay.

Eventually, my mother came home. She was in the habit of disappearing for a few days or a week without notice. She had a system of locking us in the apartment so we could not get out. My siblings and I never knew when she would be back or what state of mind she would be in. As anticipated, she was furious. Not only had I used all of her makeup; I had "ruined" the walls in the process. She beat me with a broomstick, working out her endless fury on my tiny body. It hurt, sure, but I didn't care. I had made something and I liked it. The lipstick mural was the first time I remember expressing myself, and the self-expression was positive. I had escaped the hell of my surroundings for as long as the act of drawing and the materials to do so had lasted. It felt good. I was empowered. I was happy. There was hope.

WHO AM I?

Today, the circumstances of my life have changed dramatically. I have gone from being an unknown art appreciator to opening and running a successful, multi-million-dollar art gallery in Philadelphia. In the last 16 years, I have grown through the industry on my own and emerged as an internationally recognized art dealer and consultant. I have shown and cultivated emerging artists coming out of graduate school, who were also unknown, and garnered national recognition for their work.

Since opening the gallery when I was 26 years old, I've received favorable media attention from *The New York Times Magazine* as an arts destination in Philadelphia. Tory Birch included me on her "Women to Watch in the Arts" program through her foundation for women, and I appeared on Anderson Cooper's "On the Rise" show on CNN.

Last year, I expanded my business to the West coast with an art advisory firm and have been working with private and corporate clients from around the globe. I've come a long way from that dirty tenement apartment with an abusive mother and little more than a bag of makeup as an outlet.

There is a myth surrounding the art world: that it's reserved exclusively for the elite and privileged few. A lot of people are scared of the arts because there is an aura of impenetrability. When I first encountered that aspect of the art world at my first New York gallery job, I wanted to run in the other direction. Aspiring artists think it's impossible to break in, let alone succeed or be able to support themselves. The elite segment of the art market largely supports that theory. I am living proof that it can be done.

WHY THIS BOOK?

My hope in writing this story is to inspire artists and anyone interested in working in the arts to go for it! Anyone can make it in the art world. If I've done it, you can too. I came from absolutely nothing, but with a lot of hard work, determination, and perseverance, I was able to carve out a niche for myself. There were sacrifices and periods of self-doubt and even weeks and months of fear along the way. I did not have family money or friends on the scene who could help me break in.

Despite tremendous adversity and hardship, everything I've accomplished has been a direct result of creating a vision for how I want my life to be and then manifesting it. After starting out with zero money or clients, my business is now operating out of a beautiful building that I own on Washington Square Park in Philadelphia, my artists are enjoying success, and I am deeply gratified.

If you trust yourself and listen to your inner calling, you can and will achieve your dreams. I've been tremendously fortunate that I found my true north and my center at a young age. As a child, I spent a lot of time having to be quiet. If we made noise, we got in trouble—beaten-with-a-broomstick-level trouble. This helped me to create a sense of being okay in my own skin. I became an expert at sitting quietly by myself with nothing to do except be in my own head and body. In many ways, I am grateful for this early silence because I learned to feel comfortable with myself and privately celebrate who I was on the inside. I used to say to myself over and over: this is not my life; this will not be my life. I knew there was a better life for me outside of those dirty walls. By following my intuition, I've been able to create that life for myself.

There will always be people who try to dissuade you from your path or tell you that what you're trying to achieve cannot be done. At every step of my journey, there have been people saying, "No, Bridgette. You can't. You shouldn't. That's not how it's done. You'll never make it." Some of them looked at me with pitiful eyes, or even scorn and anger. If you're facing the same type of response, ignore all of that noise and clamor. Block out the naysayers—even if they are within your own family or they are your best friends—and listen to yourself. The mistakes you will make, and the missteps along the way, are yours alone. Own them, learn from them, step and live through them to get to the other side. I wouldn't trade any of my struggles or challenges because every single one of them only fueled my determination.

This book is a personal account of my own life and experiences. Mine is a story of hope. It's about how my passion for art and creativity became a safe haven from my abusive early childhood, and ultimately sent me toward a successful career in the arts. By surviving and transforming the hand I was dealt, I've been able to persevere through obstacles both formidable and foreign, and you can too.

The terrible days do pass and truly, anything is possible if you stay focused. Setting intentional goals and visualizing the outcome has helped me achieve the unimaginable. Through living and working in the arts, I have been able to be myself and be authentic, which is a reward more valuable than gold.

I want whoever picks up this book to feel the same sense of urgency to listen to themselves as I did. We are all put here on this planet to contribute something and leave a piece of ourselves behind. My path keeps moving in the direction of a larger purpose simply by living the life I want to live. In reading my story, I hope you will find the inspiration, the courage, and the strength to find and follow your own truth because your life is waiting.

PART I

THE FORMATIVE YEARS

o n e

JERSEY CITY, NEW JERSEY

THE NEW JERSEY DIVISION OF YOUTH AND FAMILY Services (DYFS) was my government appointed surrogate caretaker from infancy until I was about eight years old. My five siblings and I bounced individually from one foster home to the next, in between stints "at home." We ranged in age from an infant to ten years old.

Our birth mother was a drug addict and an alcoholic with a handful of mental issues, none of which I ever fully understood. She crashed and raged in and out of the one bedroom Jersey City tenement apartment at random. There were times she left us alone for weeks without food, clothing, or an explanation.

Neighbors or strangers took notice of our filthy, half-starved tribe and called the authorities. We were separated and distributed throughout New Jersey to various homes within the foster care system. I was probably in 20 or more different homes throughout my early childhood starting when I was a baby.

The foster homes were creepy and crowded with other uncared-for children, many of whom were much older and very rowdy. We all had to compete for food or space and the other kids often hit me. These places were dangerous, terrifying, and always temporary. I was in a constant state of alert and often in fear for my life. After a brief period of adjustment, invariably we were returned to the apartment, to my mother, and to her rage.

Information about my mother's background is scant; my father's even more so. She was of Polish descent and we think he was Irish. I have no memory of him, which is probably just as well. When my mother was around, she was always doped up on something or drunk. Drugs and pain meds made her quiet; she'd lie around, in an out of consciousness for days at a time. When she drank, she became loud and violent and extremely physically abusive. Her go-to weapon was a broomstick, but she'd use whatever she could wrap her hands around, even if it was our throats.

There was violence outside too. The neighborhood we lived in was rough, populated with gangs and other drug addicts. At night, we heard gunshots and shouting on the streets. Anger and danger echoed off the buildings and through our paper-thin walls. It's a testament to how scrappy and neglected my siblings and I must have looked to warrant any attention from anyone. We felt a part of the landscape, like the uncollected bags of trash and discarded needles.

Our apartment was mostly empty except for our dirty, shuffling bodies. There was a mattress on the floor where we all slept in a pile and a foul couch my mother was usually passed out on. I think she had a radio. The cupboards and the refrigerator were completely bare. The kitchen had a small table and a chair. The cabinets were rusted.

On the rare occasions we had food, it was usually a jar of mayonnaise and a bag of bread. We didn't own plates or cutlery or cups. I remember being so thirsty one time, I crawled to the toilet and drank straight from the bowl. I didn't know how else to get the water into my mouth. Whatever clothes we wore were stolen from somewhere and I have no memory of ever washing.

The overall feeling in the apartment was one of silent fear. My siblings and I huddled together in the bedroom and tried to be quiet. We knew if we made any noise, our mother would come after us. We were six little people just trying to blend into the filthy walls and disappear from sight. When she wasn't screaming at us or beating us, she was either passed out or had gone out, god only knew for how long.

When my mother was gone, we entertained ourselves with whatever we had at our disposal. I found a vacuum cleaner in a closet one day and thought it was the best toy I'd ever seen. It had wheels and a long hose. With little effort, I could drag one of my siblings around on it like a go-cart. This went on for hours until eventually I broke it. I remember having a sinking feeling in my stomach, knowing what would happen when my mother found out. She came home and the broken vacuum cleaner was sitting in the middle of the floor announcing the wrongdoing.

The beating was more severe than normal this time. She hit me over the head and kicked me in the mouth with her boot. I was on the floor crying and bleeding, trying not to make a sound. My siblings sat against the wall and watched the scene in silence.

I remember the pain but also trying to be strong. I closed my eyes and my mouth and cried silently, my body racking and shaking. I was not going to let her hear me crying. I wanted to show her that no matter what she did, she couldn't hurt me, which only caused her to hit and kick more violently. She wanted a reaction, but I didn't budge. I wouldn't give her what she wanted and I held my ground. I felt an odd sense of control. The harder she hit, the more resolute and stoic I became. Eventually, she tired.

My punishment was to crawl around on the floor and pick up all of the dirt and lint with my bare and bloody hands. Even though my face was swollen and tear stained,

I found my inner strength that day and it was powerful. I held my center and was determined to endure whatever degradation or hurt she attempted to inflict. Without ever having heard the phrase "mind over matter," I was living it. The triumph back then was five-year-old me had found a sense of control in the very heart of a completely uncontrollable situation.

Despite my resolve, I always got in trouble. My natural curiosity could not be suppressed and I was constantly looking for ways to escape the misery and boredom of my reality. Even though our refrigerator was always empty, one day I discovered it had an icemaker. I dragged a chair over to reach some ice cubes from the freezer. We were playing with them on the floor when I got the idea we should throw them out the window. The game was to try to hit people on the head when they passed by. We weren't trying to hurt anyone. We were just a couple of restless, neglected kids locked in an apartment looking for something to do. We released the ice cubes and watched them drop until they hit the ground or a human target below. I remember people looking up and I would quickly pull my head back into the window to hide.

Someone must have called the cops, because the next thing we knew there was banging on the door. My mother was off on one of her benders, so we sat perfectly still waiting for whoever was at the door to go away. We were skilled at making ourselves invisible, but not this time.

DYFS caught wind of the fact there were six kids locked in an apartment unsupervised and once again we were sent away to foster homes, but not for long.

Little kids have no sense of time. We didn't have clocks or a TV, or anything with which to measure time passing except for the light of day and the darkness of night. When our mother took off, we had no idea when she'd be back or how much time had passed since she left. Sometimes it was days, others weeks. Usually after a few days, we'd start to get really hungry, which always made us nervous.

The apartment door was barricaded shut so we could not get out; but we quickly realized that the window in the kitchen with the fire escape was not locked. I guess my mother never imagined in her drug or alcohol induced dreams we would climb out of the window down the side of the building.

We devised a system to find, beg for, or steal food. We became expert trash pickers and dumpster divers. I distinctly remember finding a bottle of Gatorade one time and thinking the orange juice was like liquid gold.

One day while I was trash picking, I found a bag of buttons. We went door to door selling them for $.25 a piece. Eventually, we got enough money to buy some food and took it back to the apartment. We may have stolen a few of the items, but we bought most of it with the money from selling what we had found. The feast was absolute heaven on earth because we earned it. Necessity is the mother of invention, and this feast is my first memory of doing what I had to do to survive: we did what we had to do to feed ourselves. It is also my earliest memory of doing something "entrepreneurial" to make money for food.

Intuitively, I knew my situation wasn't right. Even at such a young age, I just knew the circumstances I endured would not define me or be my reality forever. Even though I was often in great pain from being beaten up and was scared most of the time from being abandoned, something inside of me told me there had to be more. Through the pain and fear, I continued to look for ways to be creative. I was curious and playful. No amount of punishment could quell those tendencies, even though they were exactly what continued to get me into trouble. I refused to sit silent in the corner and do nothing. I was compelled to thoroughly explore whatever was at my disposal; even if was just a bag of makeup, and old vacuum cleaner, or a tray of ice. I found relief in anything new or foreign.

My early mindset of exploration through creativity set the stage for how I would later cope with some of the challenges I faced in school and ultimately a career in the art world. I grew up planning how I would stay alive and survive a beating, or not having any food, or drinking from the toilet bowl. If that meant I had to climb out the window and scale down a fire escape and pick through the garbage, then so be it.

There was a loud voice telling me there just had to be

a better way. That voice has always spoken to me, and it still does. My inner voice and the need for creative outlets saved my life. They helped me to get through whatever pain I was feeling in the moment and push through it. I was hardwired to be resourceful, which is a trait that set the stage for some of the challenges I faced later in my professional life. Later on, the survival instinct kicked in again when I had to figure out how to survive a tough economy with a new business. Because of it, I learned to demand a life of my own creation. The pain and degradation I suffered as a child only strengthened my character, my will, and my drive to live life on my own terms.

t w o

FOSTER CARE

AT THE AGE OF SEVEN, EVERYTHING IN MY LIFE changed. It happened through a dramatic and unlikely stroke of incredible luck. I was in one of many foster homes, when DYFS caught wind of the fact that the children in the home, myself among them, were being neglected. The agency representatives swooped in to remove me and the other kids from the home, but they had to find somewhere else for us to go—and fast.

Several hours and light years away in Hunterdon County, NJ, a woman named Elaine Mayer was reading the local *Democrat* paper. She saw an advertisement from DYFS for foster care families that caught her interest. Elaine had three sons of her own, two in high school and one about to head off to college, but she wanted to help and she had always dreamed of having a little girl in her life. The advertisement prompted her to apply. Her motivation stemmed from the purest desire to give back and do something to help children in the community. Most of the foster parents I'd encountered did it for the nominal money, not to help. But Elaine was different.

Very rarely does DYFS place children outside the county of their origin. This time, they were desperate. They had removed my younger sister and me from our mother on a Thursday and they needed to find somewhere for me to go by Friday before the office closed for the weekend. If they couldn't place me, they were in a bad spot. I couldn't go back to where I'd been and going to my mother's was not an option either. Frantic, they kept widening the net and they were desperate to find a last-minute home for us. They widened the net as far as Hunterdon County. They found Elaine in the database, saw she wanted little girls, and called her. Immediately and without hesitation, Elaine said yes. She made the commitment to take us the next day without even speaking to her husband about it.

Russ Mayer worked for Bell South, which is now AT&T, in Newark, NJ. He was at the office in a board meeting when his secretary told him his wife was on the phone and needed to speak to him urgently. He was irritated by the interruption and said, "I'm in a meeting. The whole board is here and I'm holding things up. Whatever it is will have to wait." Unceremoniously, he hung up.

When he got home that night, Russ asked his wife what it was she needed to speak with him about so urgently. Elaine told him she had committed to taking in five- and seven-year-old foster girls. The DYFS woman would meet him with the two girls in the lobby of Gateway One in Newark the very next day. He and the girls were to take the train with him and then drive home. Russ knew his wife well and understood that once Elaine made up her mind up about something, she was going to get her way, regardless of what other people wanted. He was supportive and he recognized the decision had already been made. This policy of Elaine's to say "yes" and ask for permission later is something she eventually taught me, and it's stayed with me to this day.

There I was, sitting in Jersey City, tiny and scared within the system, having a completely horrible life. The DYFS agents told me they found a temporary home and we were leaving the next day.

I was used to being shuffled around. I had been in and out of the foster care system since I was an infant. It seemed like every couple of weeks, I was moved to a new house. The social workers never told you where you were going or how long you'd be there. The only thing certain during my first seven years of life was uncertainty. When I was very young, around two or three years old, I was scared of each new place, but eventually I became numb to it. The DYFS people usually just dropped me off at the new house, the paperwork was signed, and they left me to fend for myself.

The houses were always chaotic and unsupervised. There must have been ten kids at one of the places I was sent to. I remember a whole bunch of kids running around, screaming, being rowdy, and going nuts. The people had a TV, which was something we didn't have at "home," and I remember sitting on the floor in front of it, mesmerized by cartoons. One of the larger kids ran over and jumped on me so hard, he broke my arm. I was in terrible pain and ended up going to the hospital. The whole experience was traumatic and I felt like I was in a zoo.

When it was time to meet Russ Mayer, the social worker took my younger sister and me to the Gateway One building next to the train station, as previously arranged. She had a trash bag with her that had some random men's clothing shoved into it, which was meant to be for us to wear. We walked into the busy marble lobby full of executives in business suits hustling in and out of the building and waited for Russ Mayer to arrive. I was quiet and withdrawn. I kept looking down because I could not understand where I was, or why there were so many people around me dressed in funny outfits.

Russ finally came out of one of the elevators and headed toward us. He spoke with the social worker, who handed him the dirty trash bag of clothes. He looked over at us and told us to stay close to him. We followed him into a crowded train and rode to another station outside of Newark where Russ parked his car.

When I climbed into the back seat, right away everything felt different. The crowded city streets turned into a wide, fast highway and the scenery started to open up. With each passing mile, there were more and more trees and color. The drab, gray building and asphalt streets morphed into lush green grass and beautiful rolling hills and fields. Eventually we were on winding backcountry roads. I'd never been out of the city. I had barely been out of the dirty tenement buildings we grew up in. I remember looking out of the window and feeling excited.

We pulled up to a big house in the middle of a farm. As I stepped out of the back seat, two gigantic furry dogs came bounding out of the house. I had never been around dogs before and was a little afraid of them, but also a little giddy. The dogs were followed by a woman, who bent down to say hello. She looked me in the eyes and took me by the hand. I remember her eyes were an intense, piercing blue color, unlike anything I had ever seen. Her voice was beautiful; it was lyrical, angelic, and kind. I was used to my mother's voice, which was harsh and raspy from chain smoking and yelling. This new lady was utterly foreign, but in the most friendly and comforting way.

I knew the minute I met Elaine and walked into the Mayer's large farmhouse on Sliker Road, for the first time in my life, I was where I was supposed to be. It wasn't until much later, once I heard Elaine's version of the story, that I could truly appreciate how much the stars had aligned for me that day and how dramatically my life would change as a result of being taken in by the Mayers. It was one of those magical, fortuitous, crystal clear life moments that would be impossible to recreate and was precious in every way.

Immediately, Elaine wanted to make me feel comfortable and cared for. She saw I needed a shower, clean clothes, food, and a good night's sleep in a bed. I can't remember having showered or bathed prior to arriving at her house, and the feeling of being clean was a completely new experience. I arrived with matted hair and lice, which Elaine tackled without batting an eye. She used a special acidic shampoo and a fine-tooth comb. Ultimately, she wound up cutting my hair short, so she could handle the knots and the nits.

On one level, I was terrified to be in such a strange new environment and felt painfully shy, but on the other, I was ready to surrender to this woman who radiated kindness and generosity. She took me upstairs to my own new bedroom. I was coming from a single mattress on the floor shared by six kids in a one-bedroom tenement. The concept of having a bed to myself, let alone a whole room, was completely outside of my comprehension.

She opened the closet to show me what I could put on after a hot bath. I was in awe of the hangers upon hangers of neatly arranged clothes. There were dresses, skirts, jackets, and sneakers. She opened the drawers of a bureau and pointed out stacks of clean underwear, socks, T-shirts, pants, and sweaters. I could not get my head around what she was telling me. She said these were my clothes and I could put on whatever I wanted. There was a beautiful bed on the side of the room with crisp white sheets, a blanket, a comforter, and pillows. She said that was mine too. She showed me down the hall to a sparkling bathroom. It had fluffy towels, soap, shampoo, toothpaste, and my own toothbrush. There was running water and toilet paper. It felt like a dream.

The kitchen in the old farmhouse was yet another world of wonders. It was a large room with a beautiful wood table in the center with carved claw feet. The six Old English Sheepdogs that Elaine bred and raised loved to congregate in the kitchen in hopes of getting some scraps of food. There was a large white refrigerator and dark wood cupboards.

Elaine asked me what I would like to eat and opened the refrigerator. I almost fell over; it was stocked to the gills with milk and juice, vegetables, bread, eggs, and all kinds of other foods I had never seen before. She poured a glass of milk and found a jar of peanut butter to make a sandwich. At first, I was scared by it. The peanut butter was brown and slimy and smelled funny. I quickly told Elaine that I could not eat it because I might get sick.

There were so many foods I had never been exposed to: oatmeal, lettuce, broccoli, and carrots. I told Elaine I was allergic to it all. I lied a lot, because I didn't want to say or do anything that would get me in trouble. I was afraid of the newness of all of these foods and how they looked with their colors and textures. She tried to explain to me I was safe and didn't need to be afraid. She said I could try some of the foods and that I might like them. Though it would take some time before I felt comfortable, I knew that Elaine, her farm, and her family were my destiny.

Another huge event in those first few hours was meeting Elaine's three older sons. They were sweet and curious about the new little creatures in the house. I remember they were so welcoming and helpful in trying to make me feel safe. They were deeply connected to their dad and helped him with all of the chores around the farm, so they showed me the ropes.

I remember holding hands with one of the older boys. He lifted me onto his shoulders so I would not get knocked over by the dogs and carried me out into the backyard to a split-rail fence where the animals were grazing. There were horses and cattle, sheep and chickens, cats and dogs. A beautiful, brown horse named Bee came over to say hello and give us a nuzzle. We fed her a few carrots and she had a very soft nose. I had never seen an animal of that size and power. There were vegetable gardens and rolling fields and grass, a patch of lilac trees and flowers everywhere; it was a world of color and light. The land stretched out as far as I could see and turned into woods. I felt like I was in a movie or a fairy tale.

The sheer abundance of life on the farm was a stark contrast to where I had come from in Jersey City. In that place, there were trash bags and broken glass; dumpsters, cop cars, and gun shots. The more time I spent at the farm and the more entrenched I became, the deeper the internal divide became between my old life and the new. I wanted the farm to be my life forever, and I wanted to be rid of Jersey City, my birth mother, and all of the fear and pain that happened there. I clung to the new with every fiber of my little being.

I had been in the system for so long, by the time I showed up at the Mayers there was a ten-page file on me. It detailed the psychological and physical abuse I had endured and the many foster homes I had bounced between. When a family commits to foster a child, DYFS never provides a fixed time frame. They tell the foster parents and the kids the arrangement is temporary. I could have been with the Mayers for a week or a few months. No one really knew for sure, because DYFS was waiting to see if my birth mother would get clean from drugs and alcohol. No one knew how long that might take or if it would even happen.

Regardless, once a month, I had to go back to Jersey City for a supervised visit with her in one of the DYFS offices. She told me over and over again that she was my real mother. She was going to get a job and get me back. She told me my new life was temporary and I shouldn't get too used to it.

The more attached I got to the Mayers and life in Hunterdon County, the harder those visits with my birth mother became. They were scary and disruptive. They caused me to have nightmares and shut down. The last thing on Earth I wanted was to have to go back there and live that life again. Every time I returned to the farm from those awful monthly visits, I felt a tremendous sense of relief and belonging. It was as if I just woken up from a very long, bad dream and had been returned back into my real life.

Slowly, my life started to normalize. I had a shower every day and fresh clothes to wear. I had my own clean bed to sleep in and three square meals a day. My basic needs were being met; I had nutrients and clean air. No one was beating me. I started to feel some small measure of safety and security.

three

ADOPTION

AFTER ABOUT SIX MONTHS OF SETTLING INTO MY new idyllic life, Elaine came to talk to me in my room one afternoon. She explained that although she and her husband and sons loved having me and taking care of me, my mother was ready to have me at home again full time. She said the DYFS people were coming to take me back to Jersey City.

I just burst into tears. I could not process the logic of the arrangement. I was finally happy. I was healthy, I was in school and being fed and cared for. I had no interest in leaving. That was the old and this was the new. Why would the system send me back to an environment where I would be beaten up and starved by a woman who had a history of alcohol and drug use? Even though I was still very young, I was old enough to know this made no sense whatsoever. I was just starting to come out of my shell and build my new life.

Elaine could clearly see the trauma the news caused and she was distraught too. There was nothing she could do; she didn't have any legal rights and the system was on the side of my birth mother. Elaine gave me a stack of envelopes with her address and stamps on them, paper and a pen. She told me if things went badly, I should use these things to write to her. She showed me what a post office and a mailbox looked like so if I needed her help, I could send her a letter through the mail. She also wrote her phone number on a piece of clothing and taught me how to make a collect call. She had me practice the number over and over to memorize it. These small things were lifelines to reach her.

Not long after my talk with Elaine, the social worker came to pick me up and take me back to hell. Instead of the trash bag of used men's clothing I arrived with, I was being sent back with suitcases full of girl's clothes that fit me, books, stuffed animals, and toys. I even had a brand new red bicycle. All of my worldly treasures were crammed into the back of the station wagon. I climbed in and Elaine was standing on the front porch, trying to be brave as we pulled out of the long dirt driveway. I knew she wanted me to stay with her just as badly as I wanted to remain there. But there was nothing either one of us could do except wave good-bye and cry. That moment of watching her face disappear from the back of the station wagon caused me more despair than the beatings I knew I was going back to.

As I've gotten older, I've realized that even back then, I had a strong ability to walk into a room and identify the situation. If something bad was happening, or there were bad people around me, I knew it was time to retreat into myself and be as quiet as I possibly could. What I was going back to was not good and back inside my head I went.

Upon return, my birth mother immediately got rid of all of the nice things the Mayers had given me. She either threw them away, or sold them, or gave them to the other siblings. She found the envelopes from Elaine and destroyed them. Within a week's time, my mother was right back to her old ways. She was drinking around the clock and strange men came in and out of the apartment at all hours. My siblings and I hovered in the corner on the mattress and tried to make ourselves invisible. In the blink of an eye, we were all back in the old life: miserable, scared, and starving. It didn't take long for DYFS to get involved. My mother beat one of my older sisters so badly; she cracked her skull and she had to go to the emergency room.

Elaine got a call from DYFS asking if I she was interested in having me come back. Nothing had changed in my home life. All of the pain and fear she had spent six months smoothing and soothing over was back as if nothing had ever happened. She agreed to take me immediately, and it was at that point she decided enough was enough.

DYFS told Elaine she should consider herself lucky they were placing me back with her. They could put me anywhere they wanted to, and made a big deal of acting like they were doing her a favor. She wasn't my birth mother, she didn't have any rights, and she shouldn't ruffle any feathers. They told her not to get too attached. It was in that moment, Elaine realized the system saw me as no more than a number. In fact, she refers to their attitude toward child placement as "finding a dog a kennel." She realized if she wanted to have any real impact on my life and if I was going to have a chance at having a better life, she needed to adopt me legally. She set the wheels in motion to fight the system.

In true Elaine fashion, she went after it like a bloodhound. She is one of the most strong-willed and resilient women I have ever known, and very smart too. The judge who signed most of the important paperwork regarding my placement was difficult to reach directly. So, Elaine developed a relationship with his secretary. They spoke on the phone weekly, for at least an hour at a time. Elaine shared with her how unstable and abusive the conditions were back in Jersey City. She told her about my nightmares, my fears, and my progress in school. The secretary, moved by the story and Elaine's determination, took the information to the judge so he could make an appropriate decision.

I wasn't aware at the time of all the legwork Elaine was doing to adopt me, but I did know there was finally someone willing to fight for me. She asked me if I wanted to stay with the Mayer family permanently, and of course, the answer was yes. I was so lucky that her husband and sons had embraced me too. The whole family was emotionally invested in the adoption process. Finally, I was in a stable environment being taken care of and it felt good.

Years later, Elaine told me she was prepared to go directly to the New Jersey State Governor and even the White House, if she had to. Her determination and tenacity have had a huge influence on me, and I am beyond fortunate to have such a strong role model and someone who was in my corner fighting for me. I'm also proud to be like her. If we want something to happen, we make it happen. Nothing gets in the way.

To this day, I think, with wonder, what are the chances this incredible woman and her husband would want to adopt me? Who would want to adopt a damaged seven year old? She and Russ put money on the line with an attorney, she poured her energy into the fight, and she became attached to me enough to want to give me a better life. She saw she could break the cycle and provide me with opportunities I would never know otherwise.

While Elaine was fighting for adoption behind the scenes, I was facing my own set of challenges. Still very shy and scared, it was hard for me to look people directly in the eyes, and I was constantly worried about getting into trouble.

Up until I went to stay with the Mayers, I had never attended school for more than three days at a time. My birth mother kept us out of school because the administration reported our condition to the authorities, which always resulted into us being placed in foster care again. Eventually, my mother abandoned the notion of school altogether and just kept us locked in the apartment.

Elaine registered me at the local school, but having never been in a classroom setting, I struggled. I didn't know how to read at all and the school told Elaine I would have to catch up if I was going to move into the second grade. She worked with me on my reading and writing, and that first summer, Russ and Elaine hired a tutor for me.

Schoolwork and learning was very challenging for me. I had to work three times harder than everyone else because I had missed so much already. The Mayers bought me a vintage school desk and chair at a garage sale and placed it under the shade of an apple tree in the front yard.

My tutor came every day and we worked for eight hours straight. Elaine supplemented at night after dinner. I didn't give up; I just kept working. I learned how to read and write and do arithmetic. With a lot of determination and perseverance, I got through all of the first grade course work over the summer. I went to school, took the placement test, and passed. I had made it into the second grade!

Elaine and Russ were so happy and impressed that I could sit still and study for eight hours a day. The scene is emblazed in my dad's mind because he saw how hard I was trying. He had not seen a young person sit for that long for so many hours and work so diligently. I enjoyed every minute of it, even though it was a massive challenge. I had a goal and I wanted to achieve it. This is a trait that I have called upon many times in my life.

Slowly I made a few friends at school, but I always felt like an outsider and knew I was different than the other kids. Everyone was so friendly, active, and talkative! I was terrified. My social skills were nonexistent and it was hard to know who to trust. The only people I had known before were my siblings and we huddled together like pack animals to stay safe and quiet. That behavior doesn't translate to second grade social dynamics in any way.

When I was eight years old, there was a small trial with an attorney from DYFS and the attorney the Mayers hired, Mr. Mitchell. We all sat in the courtroom but I don't remember exactly what was said. I do remember the judge ushering me alone into his chambers in his big black robe. He seemed very large and intimidating. He leaned over and looked me in the eyes. I immediately looked down because I was afraid. He asked me some questions about how I liked living on the farm with the Mayers and their family. He asked me if I would like to be adopted by the Mayers and I quickly said yes!

The judge went back into the courtroom and I remember his gavel hitting the desk with a loud bang. Everyone smiled and stood up and was hugging. Elaine bent down, looked me in the eyes, and said, "Now you can call us Mom and Dad." My eyes teared up and I felt a sense of relief. I knew what that meant. I finally had a real mom and dad!

As the Mayers completed the official, legal adoption process, there was an immediate shift in my attitude from the old life to the new life. Even though I struggled in school and had a hard time fitting in, I was able to embrace my situation simply knowing I wouldn't have to go back to Jersey City. I had a beautiful family that loved me and a wonderful place to live. I have always thought of Elaine as my true mother because she loved me the way a mother is supposed to love a daughter. I was able to relax into an overall feeling of security and stability.

The farm itself was like a warm blanket. There was so much variety in the environment and in each day. It was lush and beautiful and calming. The rolling green hills and majestic animals were a rich part of the fabric of my new family life. The landscape was a 180-degree turn from my previous setting, in the poorest and dirtiest section of the city.

I started to learn how to feed and take care of the animals and help with chores around the property. My new mom raised Old English Sheepdogs and there were always at least five or six of them around. One of them slept at the foot of my bed every night, which I loved. I was starting to heal and feel empowered by my new surroundings.

When I was ten, I joined the 4-H Club. My dad had Black Angus beef cattle on the farm and I learned how to nurture an animal into adulthood, just as I was being nurtured back to life. Being outside and playing in the natural world after school every day was liberating and invigorating. My natural curiosity and exploratory tendencies were stimulated and encouraged, instead of punished.

At night and on the weekends, my dad, brothers, and I worked on the farm, tending to the animals. Everyone had chores and they changed depending on the season. On Saturdays, we collected warm eggs from the hen house and made a big breakfast with them. My dad taught me how to plant in the garden and I had my own strawberry patch. I remember digging one hundred holes and getting each one of them into the ground. Seeing and eating the fruit my hard work produced was the best reward. Gardening fostered a life long love of fruits and vegetables and gratitude for homegrown food.

As I got older, the chores got harder. In the summers, we made hay for the horses and helped my dad for 6-8 hours at a time outside. There were a few acres of large fields, several barns, a garden, and a large farmhouse, which meant there was a lot to take care of. We also helped my mom inside with the cooking and cleaning. Farm life was filled with responsibilities but it also created structure and accountability. There were certain activities that I alone was responsible for, which gave me a sense of ownership. I loved being a part of something.

One of my favorite places to go was into the woods behind the barns. I played in the forest and in the brook, collecting tadpoles and being in the quiet presence of nature. In the winters we played in the snow, went tobogganing in the fields, and built snow forts. I also loved playing in the lilac bushes in the spring and spending time with the horses, which was very calming for me. I never fully understood the healing quality of animals until much later in my life. By caring for them, feeding them, and spending time getting to know their personalities, they helped me to heal, just through their presence and our connection.

There was a solid community both on and around the farm. My parents are very social and their friends were always dropping in. There was always a buzz of activity and a lot to do, but in many ways it was also sheltered. My shyness persisted, however, and I was always the quietest person at the boisterous dinner table and didn't like to look people in the eye. My mom worked to encourage me to speak up and make eye contact, but I was still skittish.

Nevertheless, on a spiritual level, I knew I was living the life I was meant to live with my new family. All of my needs were being met and I had a consistent, fulfilling routine. I had an incredibly loving mom, dad, and family who were helping me in so many ways. Elaine was my main teachershowing me how to sew, collect buttons, exposing me to art, records, music, theater and later movies, museums, and travel. The activities and environment reshaped my young life and helped me to move past the pain that dominated the early years. Not only did my parents adopt me, I also adopted them and embraced them as my real, true family.

four

HIGH SCHOOL

WITHIN THE NURTURING ARMS OF THE MAYERS, MY life experience normalized. Once I got caught up academically with the rest of my class and became a little more relaxed in my own skin, I was able to make friends and settle into a routine. Farm life and my new family offered a level of stability. High school, on the other hand, presented a whole new set of hurdles and hiccups.

Voorhees High School in Glen Gardner, NJ was an overwhelming place. My tightknit group of grade school classmates was dismantled and discombobulated when faced with the hundreds of older sophomores, juniors, and seniors teeming through the hallways, seemingly so at home in their surroundings. I remember feeling utterly lost and nervous about so much newness.

High school presented social pressures that threatened the sheltered bubble I had become accustomed to. I started to hear about kids meeting up and having parties after school, but I always just went straight home everyday after sports practice, as was expected. My brothers were away at college by the time I was in high school, so there was more work to do. I joined the cross-country, track, and field hockey teams, and poured myself into sports. I had started running when I was 12 years old as something to do in the summers and participated in a few road races near the farm.

Toward the end of my freshman year, I started to realize my parents were really strict. How was I going to fit in with the other kids if I had to go home after school every day? I didn't realize at the time, most of the kids who were partying after school had working or divorced parents and little to no supervision. That kind of practicality doesn't matter one bit to a 15-year-old girl. I wanted to be with the rest of my friends who were hanging out after school and on weekends, but instead I had to do chores. Occasionally I was allowed to get together with friends if I finished everything I needed to do, but it was never a given and it was hard to make plans.

Once again, I started to feel like the odd man out in my peer group. Plus, I was working all the time: working on homework, working hard to excel in sports, and working on the farm. Instead of communicating my frustration (because, what teenager knows how to do that effectively?),

I reverted to my old ways of internalizing my feelings. Many times, I simply decided to do whatever I wanted, despite my parent's expectations. I started to sneak out and get into trouble. The determination to do things my own way and to fit into my peer environment, no matter what the consequences, could not be quieted.

Most of the older kids I wanted to hang out with were drinking, smoking pot, and having sex. Understandably, my mom very badly wanted to protect me from exposure to drugs and alcohol. Her unease went beyond the average parental concern. I was at greater risk due to my birth mother's addictions and behaviors. I never wanted to be anything like her; I just wanted to fit in. My mom and I never talked about her fears, justifiable though they were, in a way I could understand at the time. I just felt she was being overprotective and demanding. The more she tried to rein me in, the harder I rebelled.

I remember one argument in particular that went on all weekend. I was at a friend's house and was offered a beer. I drank two beers and went home shortly thereafter. I was exhausted because I'd had track practice earlier that day and I went to bed early. The next day, my mom she asked me if I had been drinking and I said I had. She smelled alcohol on my breath at dinner the night before. I was grounded for the weekend, and I was really upset. I decided that was it. I had had enough and I was going to run away. I grabbed my backpack and ran five miles to a friend's house. I called my parents and told them I would not be home and was moving out. The argument escalated, but eventually I went back home. That was the cycle with my parents for most of high school.

Despite the fact that I was constantly getting in trouble at home, I remained highly focused on schoolwork and sports. I was in the art and newspaper club. Because I had so many interests and demands on my time, I was able to move fairly fluidly between different groups of kids: the athletes, the artists, and the academics. Going to college was important to me too, and I knew all of my activities would make me attractive to schools. It was an odd mixture of performance versus behavior. Even though I was usually in trouble at home, my grades and sports achievements were consistent. School was a haven for me because I was not able to express how I was feeling with all of the rules at home.

My parents were worried and things were uncomfortable between us during the high school years, but I didn't feel I was doing anything out of the ordinary. If anything, I thought I was on the low end of the bad behavior spectrum compared to what some of the other kids in high school were up to. I felt in control of my decisions and the way I handled myself with my peers.

The only problem was I kept getting caught sneaking out! Our farmhouse was big and old. My parents slept on one side of the house and the kids' bedrooms were on the other. It was fairly easy to sneak in and out late at night undetected, but some of the floorboards creaked and the dogs sleeping the kitchen were a built-in alarm system.

In Hunterdon County, high school kids gathered in fields for impromptu parties and in old barns or garages. There was always something going on somewhere, and it wasn't hard to get a ride from one of the older kids. I think my mom had a sixth sense about my intentions, or maybe she was a light sleeper, because invariably I was caught on the way out or the way back into the house and would be grounded (again).

Despite my frequent attempts to escape from the house late at night, running was my main mental escape in high school. It gave me a release from stress and tension and all of my pent up emotions and frustration and it became a safety net. I loved the challenge of tackling the open roads and rolling hills on foot. My specialty was long distance and I knew all of the routes and mileage within a ten-mile radius of the house. The longer I ran, the better I got. The discipline and rigor of it gave me a feeling of accomplishment and it's remained a constant in my life. There was nothing better than running five to eight miles, being covered in sweat, and feeling amazing. I would stand in front of the fridge and eat whatever was available. I didn't need to worry about how much I ate because I was 110 lbs.

As much as running was a physical and mental outlet, art classes became a vital creative channel. My teacher,

Mr. Friend (no, I'm not kidding), opened up a whole new world for me with his curriculum. He emphasized art history and explored various artistic movements, styles, and schools of thought. He gave the class a rich context for the art projects he assigned. We were free to imagine and to create in a supportive and encouraging environment. I understood the assignments on a deeper level than I ever did with math or science. I took on AP art with the same fervor and love for expression as I did cross-country running.

Art classes became an anchor because I was good at it and it was satisfying. I explored all of the artistic mediums available in high school and loved each of them: drawing, painting, printmaking, ceramics, and sculpture. Clay and charcoal, paints and pens helped to define and articulate who I was as a person, which is something everyone is trying to figure out as a teenager.

I didn't feel the need to be competitive with art because it was something I had a natural affinity for. It offered me a haven from all of the high school baloney such as wearing the right clothes or hanging out with the cool crowd. I had an escape from all of the silliness that takes up so much energy and air space. I was different from everyone else. I learned differently, my clothes were different, my interests were different, and I felt altogether "other," no matter which friend loop I hung around with.

In the summers, my parents rented a house at Long

Beach Island, NJ. They were always on the lookout for a more permanent summer residence, and each summer we'd test out different houses and locations on LBI.

I will never forget the first time I saw the ocean. My parents were looking at a summer rental in Surf City on the bay. Afterwards, we walked across the street to the beach. I had never seen anything like it! There were miles and miles of soft, squishy sand and the beautiful waves were crashing onto the shore. I remember feeling the wind and the smelling the salt in the air. I picked up a pile of dried seaweed and ran down to the shore to watch the waves come in and out. I was instantly excited and fell forever in love with the beach. My mom was so happy for me to have this experience this and the first memory of going to the beach sticks with me to this day.

When I was around 12, my parents bought a house in Harvey Cedars on Long Beach Island. We went down there every summer and I spent hours running up and down the 18-mile boulevard that stretched from one end of the island to the other. We were three houses in from the beach and we could see the ocean from one of the decks.

Each of the rooms in the house was a specific color and my favorite rooms were the dark purple room and lilac colored with matching Levolor blinds. The other rooms were painted dark blue, red, lime green, and pink! The furniture was painted to match each of the room colors. As an artist and creative person, I loved the bright and colorful rooms as well as the feeling each one evoked. One of the rooms was called "the boat room." It had an 80s hanging fabric collage with a puffed up boat stuffed with fabric.

Most beach homes come equipped with an outdoor shower, and ours was no different. I had never experienced one before and I thought it was such a great concept. When it was dusk and cold, I would jump into the hot shower outside. It was so much fun.

Long Beach Island was the first time I ever ate seafood and shellfish. At first, these strange fish foods frightened me, but eating them was almost a ritual in my family. I will never forget learning how to eat a lobster and the fun of dipping it in liquid butter or the taste of fresh corn or tomatoes in the summer. My dad was a grill master, as were my brothers. Because we raised Black Angus cattle, there was always incredible organic farm beef to cook out at the beach. Summer meals are still a family tradition whenever I see my parents, who have now retired to their home on LBI.

I could never have foreseen it, but Long Beach Island became a critical part of my youth and my high school years. I kept myself busy in the summers working. The moneymaking opportunities for a young girl like me were everywhere. I started at the age of thirteen as a mother's helper for a woman named Ruthann from New York City who had two daughters. We became close over the years, and later she became one of my mentors when I was trying to break into the art scene in New York.

I also worked at the local grocery store, Neptune Market, bagging groceries for a few hours a week. My mom exposed me to a lot of people and taught me the responsibility of working for others. I was still extremely shy and quiet, and I know my mom hoped that being around other people would help me to come out of my shell. I was often nervous when faced with new responsibilities, but I listened well and quickly found my way.

All of the hard work in school, in sports, and on the farm had carried over to my free time. My summer jobs over the years were many and varied. I worked as a babysitter, a counter girl at the pizza parlor (I loved the free pizza and folding pizza boxes), a housecleaner, and a scooper at the local ice cream parlor. I helped out with catering and cleaning for parties and was also a waitress. At one point, I had so many requests to clean houses that I started my own cleaning business and made money hand over fist.

Those early summer jobs were the first time I was paid for my hard work and efforts, and I loved it. I used my money to buy candy, ice cream, clothes, books, and anything I wanted to. I remember the feeling of being empowered and excited and I also loved doing a great job for the people I was working for. My parents did not make me work; I just fell in love with being busy and getting rewarded for it. I was able to learn so many different skills from my summer jobs, including how to deal with people beyond my family and teachers. I was rapidly gaining my independence and enjoying it.

One time my mom asked me where I was putting all the money I was making. I opened a bureau drawer in my purple bedroom and showed her the all of the cash I had stuffed inside: crumpled up five, ten, and twenty-dollar bills. She taught me how to organize my money and helped me open a bank account.

I earned $70, $80, and sometimes $140.00 after a workday, and having my own hard-earned money at such a young age made an impact on me. These summer jobs also meant I stayed out of trouble and did things my parents approved of. There actually came a time one summer when my parents were not happy with the amount of time I was spent working! They wanted to see more of me, but I was constantly working. It didn't feel like work to me; it felt like freedom.

After only one summer, I liked it on Long Beach Island even more than I liked Hunterdon County. I didn't have long hours working in the hot fields or in the farmhouse. I still had chores to do, but it felt different and the ocean air was always so soothing to me. I was so free there: working, running, spending time with my friends, and saving money. I loved riding bikes, making art, and playing with my best shore friend, Julie, on the beach. We spent the days in the ocean and ate ice cream every night. It was a fun and simple life, and my parents were always so happy and carefree at the beach.

I will always be grateful for my summers on Long Beach Island. My mom knew she wanted to have a vacation home, and she was able to achieve her dream. She and my dad gave us countless amazing experiences during the times we spent there. When I look back, being at the beach was such a far cry from the dirty apartment I came from in Jersey City and what I had been exposed to.

Fall always came with a heavy heart, when the summer was over and it was time to get back to school. All of our beach friends would gather and say good-bye until next year and it always felt so sad. The promise of next summer gave me something to look forward to when things were tough at school.

PART II

THE ART OF
INDEPENDENCE

five

COLLEGE LIFE

BETWEEN ART AND RUNNING, IT WAS CLEAR TO ME (and those around me) that I was driven in areas where I naturally excelled and felt free. College remained a priority and I was determined to be the first person in my birth family to attend. Even though my SAT scores were on the low end, I hoped my grades and running statistics would balance those out. I had my sights set on Bucknell University because my dad and two of my brothers had gone there. The school was just the right size and distance from home to make sense, and I could not wait to get there and continue the Mayer legacy.

To my elation, I was accepted at Bucknell, but under one condition. Because of those low SAT scores, the school wanted me to take two college level courses the summer after my senior year. If I passed both classes with a "B" or higher, they would let me attend Bucknell freshman year. I was also been recruited for cross-country running, so my stats did wind up having an impact on college acceptance.

I chose English and Anthropology classes that summer and loved both of them. The track coach knew I was on campus as a pre-freshman hopeful, and he had me train all summer long with the top female runner in the school. Instead of being down at the Jersey Shore with my friends, I was training twice a day and going to classes.

Something inside of me shifted, and I was on a mission to be the best in everything I tried. I wanted to prove to the school, my dad, and myself that I deserved to be at Bucknell. I was going to make the opportunity work for me and I wanted to excel in every area. I was determined to be the best athlete, the best student, and the hardest worker on campus. I got a B and a B+ in the classes, and by the end of the summer, I was ranked as one of the top five runners at Bucknell. I was ready to start college with a bang.

People of my generation often associate the college years with an endless stream of keg parties, random hook-ups, and inebriated soirées. My experience was completely different. When I arrived on the Bucknell University campus in the summer of 1992, I was on a mission to make the most of the experience. This was my chance to design my life according to my own expectations and specifications, and I wasn't about to mess it up.

Bucknell is a small liberal arts college in Lewisburg, PA. At the time, the student population was only 2,500 students, which was roughly the same size as my high school in New Jersey. Although relatively small, I was initially intimidated by all of the new people. It always takes some time to get used to a new environment and figure out who can be trusted and how to navigate. My propensity for shyness kicked in upon arrival and it stuck around for the first few months as I slowly became more comfortable. Having my parents drop me off with my belongings and making my way to the orientation by myself was overwhelming even though I was excited. It was the first time I was going to be fully separated from my adopted parents and the reality of that set in as they drove off, and I was left to begin my adult life.

All of the angst and rebellion from my high school days were buried safely in the past. I was on my own, in a beautiful setting; ready to take on the college full force. It was both familiar, because two of my brothers went to school there and I had been there on many occasions for parents weekend, and foreign because I was alone for the first time in my life.

All of the tools I needed to create the life I wanted were right there at my fingertips. The summer of double training sessions for cross-country put me in fighting shape for the fall semester, mentally and physically. The value of the training became apparent the minute I stepped onto the field, ready to run circles around my teammates.

My first official run with the Bucknell women's cross-country team was an eight-mile, mainly uphill run. I ran the same route numerous times over the summer with my running buddy and I started to appreciate the value of preparation. I saw and felt the advantage it gave me when I was able to complete the first run as the top freshman.

I always had to fight to get As and Bs in the classroom because I found the work tedious and daunting. With running, I felt like I had more control and natural ability. I willed myself to run hard and do my best. It was challenging, but exhilarating. Being an athlete in college fed into my academic work and helped to keep me focused.

When I went to college I knew absolutely no one. I was so shy and I was still having a hard time looking people in the eyes when I spoke with them. I found adults in positions of power very intimidating, which included my college coaches and professors. The running team was a tight-knit group of athletes and it became my second family. Being on a team meant I had instant friends. We all suffered together through our daily workouts and friendships formed quickly.

I ran year round, although cross-country was my favorite out of all of the running sports. Every weekend of the school year was filled up with traveling for running competitions. During the week, we had practice every day. Indoor track and outdoor track were grueling for me and

I would much prefer running a 5K on an outdoor course to grinding out the laps for a 5K or 10K on an indoor track. However, the discipline of it gave me control over my mind and the ability to complete arduous tasks. I credit running to saving me in different parts of my life. I certainly know that being an athlete at Bucknell changed my entire college experience.

The cross-country and track coach, Art Gulden, was nationally recognized as one of the top college coaches. He imposed strict rules on his athletes for training and conduct. One of those rules was absolutely no drinking or drugs during the season, and if you were on both teams, like me, the season lasted the entire school year.

Coach had a zero tolerance policy and we all took it very seriously. He told us he had spies set up all over campus who were watching us and making sure we didn't try to break the rules. If anyone were caught, they would be off the team without exception. We were also expected to maintain a GPA of 3.2 or higher. There was no way I was going to mess with that and risk the humiliation of being kicked off the team. Plus, the team and the sport were far too important to me.

Once again, my friends were going out drinking and partying, and I was not. Only this time, it was my own choice. Without my parents around, I developed an appreciation for the impact of my own decisions. I decided the risk of getting caught drinking on campus was not worth the consequences. It was easier to follow the rules and do my best with the team and my studies.

Several years later, when I decided to quit the team my senior year, I had a lot of fun and experienced more of traditional "college life." However, I always regretted quitting because the memories of my teammates, our triumphs, and our struggles outweighed any of the fun I had that year.

My drive to succeed at school stemmed, on one level, from fear. I was afraid of failing, of letting my parents down, and of squandering a precious opportunity. My dad made it clear he would help pay for tuition if my grades stayed at a certain level. If they fell below expectation, he would retract support.

After summer school, training for the track team, and making the grades to finally be accepted as a freshman, I was grateful for the tuition assistance from my parents and didn't want to do anything to jeopardize it. As a result, I honed the study habits and work ethic necessary to maintain a high GPA. My goal was to excel in all areas of school, which included academics, sports, and art.

The agreement I had with my parents was they would take care of tuition and I was responsible for books, my car, and any extracurriculars. The money earned from working all of those summers on Long Beach Island burned up quickly, and it was clear I'd need to find a new source of income.

An opportunity presented itself midway through my freshman year at The Center Gallery (now the Samek Gallery) on campus. The pay was low and the hours were few, but I was given the opportunity to be a front desk assistant and to help with any gallery activities. This was my first job in the arts and it was fortuitous that I was able to get the job. One of the senior painting students, whose work I loved, was graduating from Bucknell and I asked her how to get a job at the gallery. Not only did she tell me how, but she walked me over there, helped me with interview, and transitioned me take over her job.

The gallery position was a coveted job because you could study while you worked, and it was a quiet and beautiful environment to be in. I was excited and relieved to find this opportunity. I loved working in the gallery. I enjoyed all of the activities and there was so much to learn. I soaked it all in: answering the phone, working on press releases, watching and assisting in hanging shows, and meeting the artists whose work we exhibited. The money I earned though, was nowhere near enough to cover my expenses and they only needed help for a few hours a week. It was clear I would need to have two jobs to survive the year.

After a little digging, I found extra work doing publicity for the theater department. It wound up being the best job of my college career and a wonderful complement to the gallery work. My work with the theater department became a huge part of my life and opened up a whole new world. My advisor was an enthusiastic, passionate, and energetic connector. I got to learn about upcoming productions in theater and dance and come up with the concepts and visuals to promote them. It gave me access to professors I wouldn't have met otherwise and areas of campus that were restricted to faculty and administration.

I was responsible for the creative development of all promotional materials, including posters, window displays, flyers, and painted banners that were distributed around campus and town. I worked on graphic design, sold tickets to the shows, and occasionally helped paint the sets on stage. The energy and enthusiasm of the theater and dance department was palpable and I loved being at the weekly meetings. I felt I belonged in that world and people enjoyed the displays and ideas I came up with.

The satisfaction of seeing an idea all the way through from conception to production was addictive. It also laid the groundwork for some of my early gallery work years later. The ability to publicize an event or an artist is a skill that came directly from my job with the theater department at school for four years. Even better, they were well funded and my hourly wage was more than what I was making at the campus gallery. There seemed to be no limit to the amount of hours needed, and the people involved in the department were incredible to work with and learn from.

Bucknell is not known as an art school, but the experience I had with the art department was unparalleled. There were five or six professors and I was fortunate to be able to study with each of them. They became almost like parents; they took care of their students and exposed us to so many different areas of the art world. Through patience and encouragement, they cultivated my interest in the arts, which was only further enriched by my job with the theater department. Because it was such a small department—I was one of only two graduating seniors with a studio art/art history major—they were able to give us full attention.

One of professors, Neil Anderson, is an incredible painter. Neil taught an evening class where I learned about conceptual art, performance art, and so many other cutting-edge ideas that would later prove to be very helpful in my business. He organized trips to New York City and Washington, D.C. to expose his students to art in big cities. It was crucial for us to see what was happening in the greater art world, and he understood that. Many years later, Neil was the first artist I signed when I opened my art gallery.

Those early art experiences fueled my desire to work in the arts in New York City after college instead of going back to the farm where I grew up. Being around the incredibly smart and active art professionals at Bucknell and who worked in the art world opened up a lot of doors.

There was a time, when I first started to look at colleges, that I thought I had to go to art school in California if I was going to have a career in the arts. It seemed like that's what all of the successful artists were doing back then. My parents said absolutely not and were adamant that I attend a liberal arts college. Years later, I know their guidance proved to be tremendously important. Being at Bucknell strengthened my mind in so many areas outside of my immediate interests, such as biology, management, and anthropology.

College was the perfect storm of independence and structure that served to solidify my increasing sense of self-awareness and unstoppable drive. The combination of athletics, arts, academics, and all of the varied people I met through the pursuit of each collided to create a fulfilling and rewarding college experience.

The track team gave me an immediate circle of friends that included kids from my own class and upperclassmen too. There were several roommates over the years who became a part of my circle and, of course, I had the art and theater communities as well. They all made for a diverse and rich network of support that carried me through the creative, academic, and athletic challenges of young adulthood.

For the first time in my life, I was comfortable in my own skin, which is not the same as being in your comfort zone. I was happy in groups and being around people, but just as happy to be by myself working on an art project. I still felt a little bit like I was on the outside looking in, and always have, but college gave me balance and self-assurance.

I was exposed to so many different scenes and people. I said yes to almost everything I was asked to do, which only enriched the experience even more. Everything was new and my life was evolving. I was free to follow my interests wherever they led, which seemed to always be to the next great thing. Saying yes opened more doors than I ever imagined it would.

In addition to my immediate college community, I was still actively in touch with Ruthann who I worked for every summer on Long Beach Island. She was an attorney in New York City and I had done extensive babysitting for her daughters over the years. I had posted a "mother's helper" sign at the grocery store I was working in and Ruthann responded. We became close over the years and she was an early mentor to me.

Ruthann knew about my love of the arts and was instrumental in introducing me to the art world in New York. During the summers off from college, I worked for her in the city and stayed at her apartment. My connection to her opened a lot of doors for me. She was well aware of the difficulties and challenges of breaking into the art world, and she helped me to think about things differently. For example, I wasn't even aware of the concept of interning, let alone that most college kids spent their summers doing that.

She arranged for my first internship at a non-profit art gallery called The Artist Space in SoHo. I spent the summer there doing front-desk work logging slides and information into their database. It was my first encounter with a non-profit for the arts and my first exposure to New York City. It was a dramatically different world compared to Lewisburg, PA or Hunterdon County, NJ. In those places, I was nestled in beautiful farmland and immersed either in the farm at home or campus life at college. In New York, I felt the excitement of being in a bustling, thriving city.

Learning about the art world in school and actually being in it in New York were polar opposite, yet complementary, experiences. In school, we dove into the ancients of art history; we pored over slides of the great works from all over the world and learned about the different schools of thought and art movements through the centuries. I had some small exposure to New York through Neil Anderson's art trips, but living there was a wildly different story. It was a new experience entirely to be able to walk into a museum on my lunch break and see the real work up close with the naked eye, and to be able to do that every day.

Summer in New York was filled with visits to the great cultural institutions in the city and I was exposed, yet again, to a whole new world. The experience, true to my nature, was very structured. I was living with Ruthann's family, spending time with her daughters in the evenings, working at The Artist Space during the days, and exploring all of Manhattan and its infinite wonders during my free time. I was open to anything and everything that came my way during my summer there.

I also got to see a very successful female business owner in action, in her element. I was impressed by the amount of work and other activities that Ruthann juggled, including her busy family. Having her as a role model planted seeds for me that would blossom years later.

After sophomore year, I got an internship at the National Academy of Design Museum on the Upper East Side. The position came with two responsibilities. The first was learning material to give tours and manage groups that came through the museum. The second was sitting in the corner of a dusty office, logging historical documents and records into the computer. There were stacks and stacks of papers that needed to be cataloged and entered into the system. Not unlike that summer under the apple tree when I learned to read and write, I sat at my desk for hours upon hours, diligently doing data entry and loving every minute of it. I enjoyed the challenge of trying to finish all the work by the end of the day. My brain was fried and dizzy when I left, but I was able to walk home through beautiful Central Park to decompress.

My third and final summer internship in New York

was for a commercial photographer. He took pictures of babies and worked on advertisements, so I enjoyed the benefits of being in and around a commercial photography studio and all that it entailed. The internship was my first encounter working with a large group of people in a small environment.

The boss screamed and yelled at me, and everyone around him. I was performing mundane tasks such as ordering and picking up lunch for everyone in the studio. I also picked up dry cleaning, sent out mailings, and cleaned the bathrooms. I happily did the work, as I wanted to keep growing and learning more about the various industries within a creative marketplace.

My tasks seemed easy enough, but I quickly learned that particular bosses have particular ways they like things done and I was often reprimanded for not doing things properly. I started to experience panic attacks at this job, which was unusual for me in a work environment, where I normally thrived on being busy.

Between the three summer internships, I covered the entire map of Manhattan and got a good sense of the different New York City neighborhoods. Ruthann lived near the Metropolitan Museum of Art and Central Park. I learned how to navigate the subway system and found new galleries to explore. The amount of things to see and do, even on a shoestring budget, was virtually unlimited.

Even though they were unpaid, art internships are

hard to come by, and mine were a hot commodity for an inexperienced college student. Each one of them gave me an intimate peek into a different sector of the art market. Between the university gallery at school, my publicity work for the theater department, the museum tour work, the data entry, the non-profit, and the photographer, my resume was extremely diverse and I hadn't even graduated from college yet. Having been exposed to the rich variety of career possibilities within the art world, I was filled with hope for the future. I just had to hurry up and graduate so I could get started and make my mark.

six

NEW YORK CITY

I DID IT! I GRADUATED FROM COLLEGE IN FOUR years, with a stellar GPA, a healthy art resume, and all the hope and excitement a young woman with a college degree about to pursue a career in the arts could possibly have. But first, some rest. It's not that I wasn't driven, far from it. I just needed a break.

After working every single summer since I was old enough to earn money, I announced to my parents that I was going to take my senior summer "off." My plan was to park it at the beach and be a lifeguard. This decision was a direct reaction to the last time had been down at the beach, working five jobs. Always prone to workaholic-level extremes, one job simply wasn't enough to pay for all the books and extra stuff needed at college. My parents complained they never got to see me and they thought I was avoiding them. Senior summer would be different.

Lifeguarding was meant to be easy street, but I was horrible at it. I'm a terrible swimmer and I was bored to tears. Sitting around all day in the sun with my eyes peeled for danger was not my idea of fun. The money was terrible and I was unmotivated after working so hard for the last four years. My mom pulled me aside at one point to let me know she and my dad were not going to support me financially come fall. They were supportive, but stern.

In truth, they were deeply worried about my future. There were thousands of other college graduates flooding the market vying for employment in New York City. My dad read the paper every day and was seeing stories about how hard it was for recent grads to land jobs in the city. He was specifically concerned about my job prospects in the art world in a troubled economy. How was I ever going to be able to support myself? They thought my challenge would be even tougher than everyone else's. Everyone knows it's impossible to make money in the art world!

I've never been a big newspaper reader and was blissfully unaware of the economic climate, but nevertheless, my parents, in typical push/pull style, prodded me to get off the beach and hit the streets. Their desire to have me employed outweighed their desire to spend time with me after four years away at school. It was almost as if they had forgotten everything I'd been working toward over the last few years. I had steadily built my resume of relevant art experience and thought I was all set.

Not one to relish sitting around doing nothing and under the gun, I started the job search in earnest half way through the summer. Even though the future was uncertain, there was nothing more to do than embrace it and make something happen. The pressure was on!

My first real job search started in the pre-Internet days back in 1996. I got a subscription to *The New York Times* and checked the sprawling help wanted section every Sunday. Most of the jobs listings were at marketing and advertising firms and required at least five to ten years of experience. Even though my qualifications didn't meet the requirements, I sent my resume in anyway. But no one seemed to be hiring, and the phone didn't ring. Prospects were looking grim. Those newspapers my dad had been reading over the summer must have been on to something.

All of the decent art opportunities were in New York, so I just had to make it work. I was living with my parents—their worst fear. My goal was to get a gallery job, which was hard to come by, but I was determined. I was pounding the pavement and scanning the want ads religiously.

Eventually, I landed an interview with a commercial gallery through an ad in the paper. I was so nervous. I had never been on a job interview before. In the past, I had always been introduced to the decision maker by my friend and ushered in the door where I then had to do the rest. This was my first time having to sell myself, which is painful for someone who is shy like me. I'm sure I was a fidgety wreck, but thank goodness my resume with the summer internships was strong. I almost clammed up when I sat down with the owner, but through the strength of my references and my experience, I landed the job.

The gallery owner was concerned about my reliability since I was commuting—five hours a day—from New Jersey. I resolved to save up the little money I earned and get a place in the city after the summer. New York is expensive! I could not believe how high the rents were, and for nothing.

The cheapest option I found was to rent a closet space in a one-bedroom apartment on the Upper East Side with a roommate. If you're broke and you want to live in Manhattan, these are the types of choices you're faced with. I found the ad in the paper, and you never know what sort of person is going to be on the other side, especially in New York.

I went over to meet my future roommate and see if the closet space was livable. We wound up hitting it off. My intuition told me she was a nice and normal person. She worked in yoga and wanted the apartment to be a quiet and peaceful place. That was just the kind of environment I was looking for, so I committed to move into her closet and begin my life as a bonafide New Yorker, living and working in the city. My dad helped me move into the city so I could start a fresh, independent life. I was still painting at the time, so all I had was a single mattress, a dresser, a small area to hang clothes, and my easel to paint on. It was tight living.

I quickly fell into a simple, if not slightly boring routine. My day at the gallery ended at 6. I'd walk to the gym, which was my one indulgence on my meager salary, go home, make dinner, and fall into bed in my closet. I didn't have many friends in the city at the time, and I certainly didn't have the money to spend on restaurants, bars, and New York City nightlife. In fact, I wasn't too interested in life in the fast lane, so I gravitated toward my familiar habits and spent a good amount of time alone in my head.

The gallery job was an incredible experience. I could not have dreamed of a more perfect first-time job opportunity in the arts, even though the pay was the pits. The late 90s was the height of the art market and I was in thick of the action. The gallery was located in SoHo, where the whole art scene unfolded during the 80s and 90s. Artist lofts were cheap and sparse in those days, and they had a ton of light-filled space. The neighborhood was filled with characters. Celebrities, eccentrics, wannabes, somebodies, and nobodies collided into a vibrant, colorful melting pot.

I loved to stand in the copy room of the gallery on my lunch break, eating a sandwich, and staring down the street to a famous diner where I often spotted celebrities. Spike Lee was a constant character in the neighborhood and I watched him the same way I watched TV: glued to the window, chomping on my sandwich, as he sat on a bench outside the diner.

We were on Green Street off of Broadway, directly across the street from the Leo Castelli Gallery. He was well known for showcasing cutting-edge contemporary art, minimal and conceptual artists, abstract expressionists, and pop. He was also famous for nurturing and promoting new art and artists. I was in Castelli's gallery every week, knew the staff by name, and was deeply inspired by the artists he represented.

There are several pieces from those days I regret not buying, but I was barely rubbing two pennies together just for the chance to be a part of the scene. I didn't have anything left over to invest but I so wished that I did. There were some exciting opportunities in those days, and I was soaking up everything from all directions. In fact, the learning opportunity alone was probably more valuable for my personal growth than any of the art on the walls.

I remember a Roy Lichtenstein exhibition of prints and paintings from his "China" series. I had a fascination with Asian art and culture and I loved these pieces. The prints were only a couple thousand dollars, which was a lot of money for me at the time. I spoke to a staff person about the cost and asked about payment plan, but there was no way to afford one. I certainly was not going to ask my parents for the money! Years later, I saw the same print I had been eyeing for just under a million dollars. There were a few moments like in New York, when I got to know all the artists and the dealers, but I couldn't buy the work.

The gallery I worked in featured a wide range of emerging and well-established artists. It had been in business for about ten years by the time I started there, and we sold everything from paintings to abstract sculpture and anything in between. There was a perfect balance of edgy and contemporary art combined with modern commercial work. We worked with a lot of writers, producers, and artists from Hollywood, and the gallery was a never-ending stream of activity and people in and out.

My job, as the front desk assistant, involved doing a little bit of everything. I handled the phones, the visitors, mailings, organizing and cataloging images for the database, writing press releases, and updating artist resumes and their images in our database. It was the perfect combination of responsibilities I had handled either at the Bucknell campus gallery or through my three summer art internships.

There was always a lot of bustle and work surrounding art openings, and I loved coordinating all of the moving parts to execute a successful reception. There were so many elements at work: marketing and publicity, client relations, curating the show, designing the announcements, and managing inquiries. Art openings attract a wide array of individuals, from the fancy highfalutin patrons to the neighborhood homeless drawn to the free wine and food. Each show and opening was a challenge and an opportunity to learn about the artist and his or her medium, which invariably led to further research and discovery.

As a quiet type, I did my work and studied the people at the openings. I quickly learned who were patrons, members of the press, or part of the artist's entourage and watched my boss to see who he focused on. I learned quite a lot about how to handle a variety of people and their respective interests simply by observing.

There were a handful of celebrities living in the neighborhood too. The first one I met was Robert Downey Jr. He walked into the gallery one day wearing sunglasses and an overcoat. It was early in the morning and we were the only people there. I didn't recognize him until he took off his glasses and inquired about one of the artists we were representing, Martin Mull. I was nervous when I came out to greet him and walked him to the back gallery to see the artist. My first star sighting and I even got to talk to him!

Occasionally, the owner of the gallery went away for weekends in the summer and left me in charge. I loved the responsibility of having the whole gallery to myself. After a few months, I started to sell, which was and still is an incredibly thrilling aspect of the business.

I vividly remember my first artwork sale in New York. We were exhibiting a young artist from Atlanta, Radcliffe Bailey. He was in his early 20s and it was his first solo show. I was impressed by is art, which reminded me of Basquiat's. At the time, I was obsessed with Reggae music and Radcliffe had dreadlocks, which I thought was so cool. He was young and shy, like me, so I felt an instant connection to him.

I read everything I could about Radcliffe and his work. One Saturday morning, a new collector came into the gallery who was thinking about buying some of Radcliffe's works on paper. With great enthusiasm, I told her everything I knew about the work and she decided to buy two pieces. What a thrill! My boss was over the moon when I told him two works had sold. Slowly, he started to increase my responsibilities.

My intention was to learn as much as I possibly could about every aspect of running the gallery. My thirst for knowledge and best practices served me well at the time and what I learned there still informs many of my decisions today. I soaked it all in. If there was a mailing that needed to go out, I figured out and systemized the fastest, most efficient, and effective way of getting it done. I applied the same enthusiasm to press releases, and learned how to publicize shows and artists with the press.

There was a formula for each task associated with the position, and I loved figuring out the best way to do something and implement it. The exposure to a variety of mediums such as contemporary mixed media paintings, sculpture, and photography fueled the learning process.

I was slowly meeting and being exposed to some of the most talented contemporary artists, most of them who are still working today. The artists were central to the business of course, so I spent a lot of time reading about them and their work and listening intently when they talked about what they were up to.

The better understanding I had about the commercial side of the gallery, the more I began to see some of the ugly sides of the business. Still very young and naïve, the superficiality and materialism of the art world started to reveal itself. My interest and passion were for the artists and I spent hours with them in their studios, learning about what drove them and how they approached their work. People came into the gallery and bought art because they thought it would like nice in their bathroom or over the couch.

To many of the buyers, art was about decorating, instead of about the artist or the history behind a piece. Some of them only bought because a critic found favor or they saw something in a magazine. I found this attitude discouraging, but there were some valuable lessons to be learned about what motivated people to buy art. Unfortunately, there were only a few clients who purchased out of a passion for the artist and made decisions beyond being in the art club.

Because of my involvement with the bookkeeping side of the business, I was exposed to a common financial practice among galleries. When we sold a piece of art, we held onto the money for anywhere between 90 to 120 days—and sometimes longer—before paying the artist for their work. Even though this was standard procedure, it didn't sit right with me. I was friendly with the artists and they started to call me and ask when they could expect payment on the sale. Under no circumstances was fielding this line of questioning part of my job and it made me uncomfortable.

My boss instructed me to simply tell the artists their payments were forthcoming and put them off. Meanwhile, the money from art sales was used to pay bills and other overhead. Years later, when I had my own gallery, I vowed never to hold onto money and keep it from the artists. I am committed to making sure they are paid the day a payment processes and it surprises me that this is still not common practice, especially in New York.

After a few months, my life of near-poverty in New York started to weigh on me. I was living in a closet making $12 an hour. I couldn't do anything outside of my routine and there was zero extra money to have any fun. Working hard is in my nature and I love to hurl myself into new experiences and projects, but having nothing to show for it was getting me down. The necessity of getting a second job was looming.

My parents, teachers, and friends had warned me about just this scenario. They said it's impossible to make money in the arts; you're never going to be financially stable; New York is the most expensive city to live in the country. If living in New York and working in the art world meant barely getting by, as everyone had told me, I started to think it wasn't the life for me. My choices were to get a restaurant job and work seven days a week or change my situation.

The best and most immediate solution was to talk to my boss and ask for a raise. My arguments for making more money were solid. He felt comfortable leaving me alone in the gallery and managing things when he was away, I was doing way more than he had originally hired me to do, and I deserved to be compensated. Nevertheless, asking for things is hard for me and he was adamant there wasn't any extra cash for a raise.

We were in a standoff. I wasn't going to leave the conversation without something. We sat in his office, staring at each other, neither one of us budging on our position. After what felt like an eternity, he finally relented and agreed to bump my wage up to $14 an hour. Even though it was a small victory, it still wasn't quite enough to make a dent.

I started to feel like my parents and everyone had been right when they said it was just too hard to make it in the art world. Maybe it wasn't the best career path for me. How would I ever have enough cash to justify the hours I devoted to it? I loved the work and the exposure to artists, but the possibility of going down a different path started to percolate. At Bucknell, I had considered going into teaching and the idea was still in the back of my mind.

While I grappled with my circumstances and my options, I jumped on any opportunity that presented itself to make some extra cash. One of the artists we represented at the gallery asked me to look after his six miniature Mexican dogs while he was in Arizona for a residency. The assignment lasted for several months, and it seemed simple enough to feed six dogs twice a day. The artists and his wife lived in a huge, beautiful loft in Alphabet City, which was a horrible neighborhood at the time. Drug addicts and prostitutes littered the sidewalks and it was scary going back to the loft at night, in the dark, after work. I'd get inside and lock the door and stay in for the night.

One of the dogs was very old and near death. The artist and his wife had devised an elaborate feeding process to separate the older dog from the rest of the pack when it was dinnertime, so he was able to get his food without the other dogs stealing it from him. One night, shortly before the artist and his wife were scheduled to return to the city, I fed the dogs as usual. I went into the kitchen to heat up my own dinner, and immediately heard horrible, angry barking and screeching. All of the dogs had descended on the old one and were trying to tear him to pieces. There was blood everywhere. I managed to pull the old dog out of the jaws of the others, wrap him in a blanket, race down the stairs, find a cab, and get him to a local pet hospital.

After examining him, the vet said the dog had to be put down. He told me the dog was in such bad shape, it would be inhumane to treat him. I was distraught by this news. There was no way to get in touch with the artist for his permission, and the weight of the decision to euthanize his dog was more than I could bare on my own. I called my mom, who bred dogs, and explained the situation. She was in agreement with the vet; the dog had to be put down, there was no other option. It was a wretched predicament. Upon the advice of the doctor and my mother, I had no choice.

The artist was a good friend of the gallery owner. I was terrified I was going to get into trouble and possibly even lose my job over the incident with the dog. The next day, I told my boss what happened, and he was empathetic and supportive. The artist and his wife, on the other hand, went ballistic. I explained the horrible situation to them when they got home. They felt I behaved irresponsibly by making a decision of that magnitude without their consent. They were traumatized by the loss of their beloved little dog, and in turn traumatized me for how I handled the decision. The artist refused to speak to me ever again, even when he came into the gallery. It was terrible.

The incident with the dog was the first in a string of negative experiences in New York. The art scene can be snotty and pretentious. I started to be more aware of the sense of entitlement and privilege stemming from the clients at the gallery. People assumed because I was there that my parents were wealthy art collectors and that I had paid my way into the job. Their attitude was off-putting and left me feeling hollow and frustrated. All signs were pointing to the fact that it was time to start exploring new options.

A good friend of mine was contemplating moving to Taiwan for an engineering job and suggested I come along for the ride. Asian culture had always been of interest to me, ever since I studied art history in college. As fate would have it, the Leo Castelli Gallery was showing Roy Lichtenstein's "Fathers of the Past" China series at the time my friend approached me about making a move. I was in love with the prints and went to see them at least twice a week while the show was up. The colors and the landscapes Lichtenstein presented seemed to be beckoning to me.

I did a little digging and there appeared to be a wealth of opportunities to teach English in Taiwan. Museums and hospitals were paying between $25 and $50 an hour. The cost of living in Taiwan was only around $3 a day. I could live like a queen, have access to a whole new culture, and travel. The writing was on the wall; I had an undeniable chance to reboot my life and explore a new part of the world. With intuition as my compass, I was ready for a new adventure.

seven

TAIWAN

THE PLAN TO LEAVE NEW YORK AND MOVE TO Taiwan was not met with enthusiasm by my family. They couldn't understand why I would want to leave New York when I had finally gotten a raise and was doing what I had set out to do. I had been in New York for a year, which felt like a lifetime to me. They wanted me to stay for another year to build my resume more. They also thought teaching English, so far away, was a violent departure from the career path I had set for myself. There was no way I could get them to see the decision as a good one and once again, I was at a divide with my parents. They made it clear they would not help in any way and I was on my own.

As much as I didn't want to disappoint them, I knew in my gut that going to Taiwan would change my life and my perspective in ways I couldn't even imagine. I wanted to leave the United States and experience another culture. When I was at Bucknell, I had the chance to study abroad in Florence, Italy and it opened my eyes to so many things, besides the incredible art history there. One of my goals was to eventually get married and have children. My reasoning was that it would be far more difficult to pick up and take off for a year or two when I had a family.

The art scene in New York had left me feeling disillusioned, despite how enriching and informative the gallery experience had been. Many of my college friends were in similar positions in their new jobs. Some were already contemplating a career change after only one year in their jobs. I knew I needed to trust my instinct and if it wasn't right, I could come back to the United States and my family anytime.

My preparation for leaving included several visits to the Asian consulate in New York. They helped me solidify a work visa. The plane ticket was booked and temporary housing arranged. I was nervous about the language barrier and intimidated by the complexity of Mandarin; learning to communicate would likely be my biggest immediate challenge. My friend and I were excited to have independent experiences, but to lean on each other for company.

True to my nature, I spent a lot of time alone when we first arrived in Taipei, Taiwan. I enrolled in art classes and had a great job. Honestly, aside from the language and the architecture, my early days in the city were very similar to how they had been in New York. The concentration of people and my daily routine were familiar, but the culture was utterly foreign, new, and exciting. My mission was total immersion.

Unfortunately, soon after arrival, I started to get sick frequently. There was so much pollution in Taiwan and China in 1997 and there were no emissions controls in place. The sky was almost black at all times of the day. There were thousands of cars and motorcycles everywhere, spitting out black soot into the air. Taipei was one big construction zone. Buildings were going up right and left. There were concrete structures and rebar everywhere. It was noisy and filthy, but despite all of that, thousands of people traipsed through the development on a daily basis.

I noticed right away that people wore surgical masks outside in the mornings and the evenings. These were the highest commute times when the air quality was at its worst. My colleagues and friends said I should wear one too to protect my lungs. I ignored their suggestion and within a few weeks, I was coughing and run down.

The city of Taipei was chaotic, dense, and fast-paced. The volume of American fast food chains everywhere surprised me. There was a McDonalds or a KFC on every corner, just like in New York. I had expected there to be more of an old world flavor to the landscape. But, the economy was growing quickly. Taipei was a city in a race toward modernization and westernization.

The people I encountered at school through my job and within the community were highly interested in native English speakers. I was a foreign anomaly to them with my light skin, blonde hair, and blue eyes. Even strangers on the street were fascinated. Some of them boldly walked up and started touching my hair. At first, the attention was unnerving, but I realized they had never seen anyone with my fair features, which were a stark contrast to their dark hair and skin. After a while, their curiosity became humorous and endearing. Plus, it was a unique way of meeting people.

Within a few weeks, I started to travel on the weekends to different parts of Taiwan and over to Mainland China. My goal was to get to know the country inside and out. Once out of the city, there were incredible natural landscapes to explore. It was very easy to get around on buses and check out different towns and cities.

Job opportunities were not hard to come by. Everyone wanted to learn how to speak English. The Taiwanese were deeply interested in American culture, and any American passing through the area was considered a hot commodity. I was no different. As an added bonus, most of the other teachers were male. Being a woman helped me to get even more offers. The money was pouring in. I was making between $2,000-$3,000 a week. It was the most financially lucrative situation I had even been in. I went to the bank every week and deposited wads of cash and was excited to finally be building up a nest egg.

I worked at a high school, an elementary school, and I did private tutoring for juniors and seniors applying to college. It was the first time in my life that I worked with children and I loved being around their youthful, precocious energy. We connected immediately through one-on-one sessions. They were fascinated by this strange blonde American in their midst and they tried so hard to learn. You could see the effort on the faces each day.

The community of other teachers was strong and people, in general, were very welcoming. I started to relax into my environment, which is much easier to do when you have some cash in the bank and you aren't working seven days a week. Things started to open up for me and I was hungry to learn everything I could.

There was an incredible museum not too far from the school where I taught. I spent about two or three days a week there, soaking up the Taiwanese style of contemporary painting, the culture, and the rich history. I was also fascinated by Aikido and started to study and practice the ancient martial art in my free time.

Through some of the teachers I knew from school, I met a nice couple who were interested in starting their own English-speaking school in southern Taiwan. They invited me down to their house for the weekend to talk about helping them. Their house was incredible and right on the coast, only a few hours from Taipei. It was clear they were quite wealthy, but they weren't pretentious about their money the way most of the people I encountered in New York and San Francisco had been. They took me out for beautiful meals and gave me a thorough tour of the area, which was lush and peaceful. I was enchanted by this part of the island.

For the first time in months, I was able to breathe freely because the air was significantly cleaner in southern Taiwan. Being sick all the time in Taipei was starting to get me down. I worried about permanent lung damage from breathing in all the toxic fumes.

Aside from the fresh air and beautiful landscape, the couple offered me significantly more money to help with opening the school than I was making through my jobs in Taipei. They knew several people in the area who would happily pay me $100 an hour for private English lessons, which meant even more money to travel. Plus, southern Taiwan is famous for its pristine beaches, and I wanted the chance to explore them.

Ultimately, the couple's offer, the air quality, and the opportunity for further cultural immersion were too good to refuse. I committed to the couple, to helping them build a school, and to moving to southern Taiwan.

Again, my parents thought I was nuts. We weren't in frequent communication, and they were still upset about my decision to spend time in Taiwan, but I kept them posted on my whereabouts. I chose to not tell them about the pollution and my coughing, as I knew that would only worry them more. With my decision to move south, they were thrown for another loop. They could not understand at all why I wanted to be in such a remote part of the world, and why I couldn't sit still and focus on a career.

They were right; I was very far away from home, but I was making money hand over fist, I was immersed in a new culture, and I was living my life for myself. Regardless of what I was doing, which happened to be extremely positive and rewarding, I was creating my own experience and responsible for my own decisions. It made me sad they could not see the value in what I was trying to do, but thank goodness, their disappointment didn't deter me from the next adventure or living life on my own terms.

I stayed in southern Taiwan for close to a year. From there, it was easy to travel to Hong Kong, which I did several times, and Indonesia, where I spent a few weeks. I took full advantage of the opportunity to bounce around Asia whenever I had free time. There was no shortage of work either. Everyone wanted to learn English. I was a tutor for a family and worked in a high school teaching a class with a hundred rowdy boys. There were so many kids in the class; I needed a microphone to address the students, which was hands-down my least favorite part about teaching. I was uncomfortable being the center of attention and speaking in front of large groups, whether they were kids or adults.

The culture and landscape in southern Taiwan were vastly different than Taipei. It was more rural, there was more poverty, and the people, on the whole, were considerably more curious in nature. Many of them had never left the area. In some regard, it reminded me of Hunterdon County. Foreigners were a rarity and I was treated a little bit like a celebrity. People invited me into their homes for beautifully prepared meals. We sat around the table for hours trying to learn each other's languages. They simply liked hearing me speak English to get a feel for how it sounded.

There was a vast economic divide in the countryside. Some of the indigenous people and members of the lower class were living in extreme poverty. This was the first time I was exposed to people begging for food and sleeping on mattresses on the floor since I had been rescued from my own poverty back in Jersey City. I felt a certain amount of guilt about my situation. Some of the people on the streets looked like they were starving, and I was making $100 an hour to teach people how to speak my native tongue.

Many of the Asian students I worked with dreamt of going to an American college. It was humbling to realize how much privilege had been bestowed on me. As a white woman from an impoverished background, I had been adopted into a loving family and given the opportunity to go to college. I started to more deeply appreciate some of the things I had been taking for granted.

It's usually not until they leave the United States that people think about what it means to be an American. In Asia, I started to see my own country from an entirely different perspective. The people in southern Taiwan and even Taipei saw the United States as the golden land of opportunity, wealth, and celebrity. Their favorite past time is karaoke and they absolutely love American pop stars. They thought that since I was from America, perhaps I knew Elvis and hung out with him. My karaoke skills, then and now, were unimpressive, but simply being from the United States was enough to carry some clout.

Asian culture is traditionally one of conformity, so they were fascinated by our culture, music, art, and especially fashion. Most people wear uniforms to school and to work. Women tend to embody traditional roles of being wives, mothers, and housekeepers. An independent woman traveling alone, without a man, was a new sight and concept for them. While I was fascinated by the history of their culture, their art, their embroidery, and their silks, they were fixated on fast food and freedom. In their minds, the two went hand in hand.

Through my involvement with building the English speaking school, I was able to meet a lot of people in the community. Once the school was up and running, we expanded our course offerings to professionals in the area. I started doing outside contract work and helped local businesses design and deliver presentations to American companies. I taught the basics of business communication and even had a job at the local hospital.

It was at the hospital I met a wonderful family with two young daughters. They wanted their girls to be around me and learn as much English as possible. The family hired me to teach classes at the hospital and invited me over to their home for several wonderful dinners. On the weekends, they loaned me their car anytime I wanted to use it so I could explore the area. It was the first time I had experienced the generosity of this kind outside of my own family.

Through my involvement with people in the community, I was better able to immerse myself in all aspects of the culture. One of my favorite things to experience was the food. Prior to being in Taiwan, I had only ever had Americanized Chinese food, which bears almost no resemblance to the incredibly fresh and wild cuisine I tasted over there. The open-air markets offered a rainbow of sights and sounds. They had chicken feet and fish eyeballs and every kind of vegetable under the sun. Specific foods carried deep symbolism and health benefits, which was all tied into their rich food culture.

In southern Taiwan, the seafood was abundant because we were surrounded by ocean. I had never been a huge seafood fan, but I fell in love with fish. The Taiwanese were amazing cooks. Everything was steamed in bamboo baskets and highlighted the flavors of the food—fish straight from the sea, farm-grown vegetables, and green tea. I learned how to make dumplings, and soups, and rice the correct way.

On one memorable evening, the couple who owned the school took me and a few of their friends to a high-end seafood restaurant, where the specialty of the house was a whole grilled fish. They insisted I try it. This fish arrived—eyeballs, bones, and all—on a massive platter. I had no idea how to approach such a thing and there were no forks on the table, only chopsticks. Utterly out of my depth, my hosts graciously taught me how to hold and use the chopsticks. The meal ended up being both delicious and a ton of fun; everyone got a kick out of watching me try to navigate the whole fish.

At one point, the woman looked over at me and announced, "You are someone who is going to travel the world and go far from home." I asked her how on Earth she knew this and she explained that the way someone holds their chopsticks reveals their personality. Someone who holds them close to the base is a family-oriented person who will stay close to home, and someone who holds them closer to the top, like me, will travel and explore. They have the confidence and courage to try new things.

I loved the meaning behind everything in Taiwanese culture. Everything, from how you held your chopsticks to how you arranged your furniture, held significance and symbolism. I was exposed to the concept of Feng Shui for the first time, and was drawn to the "art of placement." Many of the houses had water fountains inside or out, which represent prosperity and money flow. The paint colors and furniture were chosen with care to create a peaceful and harmonious environment. Their whole approach to design is founded on simplicity, cleanliness, and organization. It's the polar opposite of what you find in most American homes: clutter, closets overflowing with junk, and stuff everywhere.

The sensibility of simplicity resonated for me. To this day, I still travel light and keep my possessions down to the minimum. My detachment from tangible objects is probably a remnant of my early childhood when I had absolutely nothing to hold on to, look at, or play with. It was so interesting to me that I would be attracted to stark and bare settings, but I loved the order and the clean style. A lot of cultural emphasis was placed on flow: the flow of life, the flow of money, the flow of spirit, the flow of your house, and the flow of your body. Eastern philosophy and spirituality is centered on the concept of energy transference, which was a concept that infiltrated every single aspect of the culture.

After just over a year of being in Taiwan, I started to get homesick for the United States. I had accomplished what I set out to accomplish. I had experienced a new culture, traveled, broadened my horizons, and saved a lot of money. The disconnect from my friends and family was becoming too hard to bear. We only communicated through letters, which took forever to arrive. The idea of leaving and heading home started to percolate.

At the time, I was running a lot at a track near my apartment. The cleaner air in southern Taiwan was better for exercise than it was in Taipei and I needed to clear my head. I loved my evening runs when the day was over, and I could process everything that was going on in my mind and blow off steam. There were always a lot of people out walking after dinner taking in the cooler night air. The small town I was living in didn't have too many runners, and I got used to people watching me run laps on the track or around the town.

On one particular night, my goal was to do five miles, which was 25 laps around the track. I started just before dusk at dinnertime. There were a handful of people out walking and there were a few people sitting in the bleachers. As the people trickled off the track back to their homes, I noticed a man sitting in the bleachers smoking a cigarette, which was a pretty normal sight. I am always aware of my surroundings when I'm running, so I noticed with curiosity the man kept moving to different areas as I made my laps around the track.

When I was finished, I was hot and sweaty and felt great. I had accomplished my goal. I hopped on my bicycle and rode back to my apartment in the dark. A man flew by me on a motorcycle, and I thought it might have been the man from the track. I didn't think much about it at the time because there were motorcycles everywhere.

As I was locking my bike up in the courtyard, someone ran past me into my apartment building. I remember thinking it was strange because Taiwanese people do not run; they walk slowly with intention. I was usually the one running. I figured I would simply get into the elevator, get up to my apartment, lock the door, and everything would be fine.

I hit the button for the fifth floor and the doors closed in front of me. I was alone in the elevator as it started to rise. Almost as quickly, it started to slow, indicating the elevator was stopping on the second floor. In an instant, I knew what was happening. The man who ran past me was going to jump out and attack me. I braced myself and prepared to put up my fists and scream bloody hell. My heart was beating quickly and my adrenaline was pumping from the run and from my fear.

The elevator doors opened and the man lunged at me. My fists were up to protect my face. I put one of my legs up, kicked him as hard and I could karate style, and started screaming at the top of my lungs. He dropped his arms, stared at me in fear, and the turned around and ran down the staircase. For some reason, my instinct was to run after him. It was a large building and I thought I might be able to get some help or the license plate of his motorcycle.

When I got to the courtyard, he was already speeding off on his motorcycle and I didn't catch the plate number. There was no one in the courtyard, but a woman on the first floor parted her curtains and peered outside. With all of my screaming, no one came out to help or see what was going on. I was upset and started crying uncontrollably. I was frightened but I was also angry at myself for ignoring my instincts, which told me something was off about this man back at the track. I promised myself I would never do that again.

When I caught my breath and stopped crying, I called my boss and asked him what I should do. He came to pick me up with his wife and they took me to the police station. I was there for several hours, filed a police report, and gave them the little information I had on my attacker.

I felt like a target and did not know what to do. I realized the person who attacked me was freely roaming around the community and I would never know who he was. My boss suggested that I move into a new building and with a doorman. I moved the very next day, with his help. He and his wife were distressed about my experience and embarrassed that someone in their country would try to attack me. My experience in Asia was coming to an end, but I didn't want it to be because I was run out of town by some crazy man. I couldn't ignore the sign, though; it was time to go.

eight

SAN FRANCISCO

THE DECISION TO LEAVE TAIWAN, MUCH LIKE THE decision to leave New York, felt fated. The stars aligned once again to point me toward a new path. Art was on my mind, just as much as ever. It was time to get back to the States, but I couldn't face going back to New York. California seemed to be the next logical stop. I'd wanted to go there for art school and the allure was still strong. I rationalized California was closer to Asia than the East Coast.

Much to my parents' chagrin, I flew straight to LA and made a mental commitment to live in San Francisco for a year. Again, my parents were unhappy with the decision. They thought I was running away from home and avoiding them. My mom had family in San Diego and Del

Mar, but had not spent time on the West Coast in many years. My dad always thought California was a place for liberal, pot-smoking hippies to hang out. He thought I was wasting my time and my life going there. The truth is, the decision to be in California had nothing to do with them.

I was still in the mindset of wanting to do all of the things I had dreamed about. Those things might be harder for me to do the older and more I established in a career I became. They might even become impossible when I got married and settled down. The early 20s are a meant to be a period of exploration and discovery, and I intended to maximize my youth and status to its full potential.

My parents came from the generation of staying in the same job from beginning to end and retiring with the same company. I'm from the early Internet generation. Although it was still unusual to jump from job to job every year or two, I was in exploration mode. I knew my potential and I knew that with hard work, I could always generate jobs and opportunities for myself. I had made a lot of money in Asia and was coming home with savings for the first time in my life.

The money I earned in Taiwan allowed me a cushion to take my time and figure things out without pressure in San Francisco. My savings were enough to cover a plane ticket, a deposit on an apartment, and a few months of living expenses. I was rich compared to the New York days. I had always had a romantic vision of living near the Golden Gate Bridge and riding trolleys, and now it was about to happen.

Life fell together beautifully for me in San Francisco. I stayed in a hotel for the first week and quickly found a house with a few roommates on 23rd Street and California, right near the Presidio. The house was owned by an Asian man, which I interpreted as a good sign. I had a big beautiful bedroom and my roommates were great. One of them worked for the anthropologist, Jane Goodall, and travelled all the time.

Shortly after finding a place to live, I was hired as a project manager at one of the top architecture firms in the city. It was owned and run by two principal partners with a handful of younger male architects. The firm was close to my house in the Presidio and the pay was great. Within a week of arriving in San Francisco, I was already set up with a job, a healthy income, and a great living situation.

It was a relief to be back amongst English speaking citizens and to have full access to American food and be relaxed and in my own country. I was so excited and confident being in a new city and excited for what lay ahead for me.

I loved being in the Presidio, right near the beach and Golden Gate Park. I got back into running with a vengeance and was logging between five to ten miles a day exploring my new city on foot. I dusted off my old college workouts and stated training in earnest. Sometimes, I ran before *and* after work.

San Francisco was the first community I lived in that embraced health and fitness. New York in the 90s was not a fitness forward city and running wasn't an option in Taiwan because the pollution was so terrible. It felt amazing to embrace nutrition and exercise again. I joined the YMCA and started to practice yoga for the first time. I bought a bike and used it to get to and from work and rode through the park and the city on the weekends. There were an endless amount of things to do outside in and around the city.

As much as life fell together neatly in California and I was excited, I experienced a radical reverse culture shock coming back to the United States from Asia. Psychologically, the transition was intense, profound, and completely unexpected. In Taiwan, I had enjoyed an almost celebrity-like status. People gravitated toward me and wanted to learn from me. I was well paid and sought after. The school provided a sweet and innocent environment centered on learning and growth.

Back home, I had to prove myself in a male-dominated, high-profile architecture firm. We were working with extremely wealthy, powerful CEOs and business tycoons. It was a serious environment and required extraordinary organizational acumen and confidence on my part. It was a cold and competitive environment and I felt very insecure and unsure of myself, especially as the only woman in the firm. It took some months to get my feet on the ground.

Part of my new job was to prepare diagrams and publications related to the work the architects were doing and present them to my colleagues. The prospect of public speaking had never been appealing. I experienced extreme anxiety speaking in large groups or giving presentations, both in college at my teaching job in Asia. In the professional environment, my fear manifested as crippling panic attacks. If a presentation was looming, or I needed to get up in front of a group for any reason, I'd have to go to the bathroom and do some deep breathing exercises to calm myself. This method was not terribly effective.

I will never forget the first company luncheon. The partners took me to a four-star restaurant to welcome me to the firm. There were eight of us around the table and I could barely look up or pick up my fork to eat. My face was hot and I was quiet and nervous. I was surprised and discouraged by the scenario, and a little scared because I wasn't sure what was causing me to feel that way. I'd been nervous before, but I had never felt so panicked. I mentally pushed through the lunch and was relieved to get back to my office and get back to work.

Unfortunately, the panic started to become a reoccurring pattern. The attacks were so debilitating and uncomfortable; I tried to avoid situations that might provoke the overwhelming feeling of anxiety. Being in groups speaking and giving opinions was part of my job.

I was reminded of sitting around the dinner table at the farm growing up and trying to disappear so I would not get into trouble. The worst part of these moments was that my face would turn bright red, and everyone could tell I was nervous, which of course, only made me turn more red and feel more nervous.

I had several bosses, all of whom were extremely creative and talented, but they had high expectations and had an air of entitlement about them. The clients fell into the same camp as the partners. I felt very much like the low man on the totem pole, because in truth, I was.

It occurred to me, probably for the first time in my life, I wasn't on the same life level as the architects I worked for. Their status was higher than mine. I started to think about how I might be able to boost myself up a few notches, even though I knew I would never behave the way they did. Entitled is a state of mind I had never experienced, and it seemed unlikely that I ever would. I didn't want to act that way, or treat anyone else that way either.

I decided to take the bull by the horns and learn everything I could about every client, every detail of their projects, and every aspect of the work. One of my responsibilities was to maintain a large architectural library and to add content and pull books related to specific projects. I made it my duty to learn that library inside and out. Over the course of several weeks, I took every book off the shelf and reorganized it. My colleagues thought I was nuts but

I was on my own private mission.

I read a few articles about professional growth and realized I needed to change my appearance to be taken more seriously with the clients and at the firm. I invested in a few suits and matched my clothing palette to the company logo and the colors of the office. I cut my hair to look more professional and my boss and the other partners took notice. Despite my previous hard work, it took a while to understand that I needed to put some effort into myself too. I started to read about business communication, including how to speak on the phone more effectively, how to be more organized, and how to win friends and influence people (Dale Carnegie).

Being at the firm was an interesting, but definitely challenging, time in my career. It forced me to confront the poverty that I had endured in my early childhood in Jersey City followed by being raised in a middle class household in Hunterdon County. Suddenly, in San Francisco, I was confronted with another stratosphere of wealth and affluence. I was surrounded by extremely powerful and influential people. Their level of success didn't seem attainable to me, although I did aspire to have more money and be able to afford nice things.

We worked on five- to ten million-dollar homes. I sat for hours in interior design and custom furniture and woodworking meetings, and got familiar with the properties. I ran through some of the neighborhoods we were working and was enchanted by them. I thought about how much I would love to have an architect design a beautiful home for me, but I was turned off by the superficiality of the world I was in and the attitudes of the people I was around. They were not humble and the arrogance was off-putting.

The culture of the firm was unlike anything I'd experienced previously. Over the course of my time there, and the more I felt comfortable, I continued to identify areas of the business that would benefit from a new or improved approach. When I tried to present my ideas, I was told to, "Pipe down my motivation level." This reaction came as a complete shock. Never in my young professional life had I been told I was too motivated. I was confused by this and realized later on that the response was most likely a result of the pot smoking that was part of the culture there after hours. My naiveté was evident, and I started to think perhaps I was in the wrong environment to boost my status.

The experience caused me to realize just how embedded an East Coast mentality of ambition was a part of my psyche. I wanted to try new things and reach new heights. My motivation was what led me to work all day and go home to a ten-mile run; to slog it out living in a closet in New York so I could learn about art; to travel to Taiwan and embrace a new culture. My intuition told me it was time to start looking for another avenue of professional development, in the arts, where I could excel and grow.

I started looking around for gallery jobs and found a non-traditional gallery called Mexit near Fisherman's Wharf. It specialized in Mexican art from the Oaxaca region, and I started working there on the weekends. The owner was a fascinating woman who travelled all over the poorest parts of Mexico to discover new art. She met with the artists and artisans to learn about their craft and brought their work back to San Francisco and put it in a beautiful gallery setting. I learned about Oaxaca handicrafts and some of their craft-making processes and then got to educate other people who came into the store about it. I was also learning how to transact a sale, wrap the work, and ship it; all of which would come into play later when I had my own gallery.

The gallery owner insisted that everyone who worked there take a one hour, paid lunch break, to reboot and rejuvenate. She believed in nurturing her staff and was generous with her knowledge and her expertise. It was a calming and pleasant environment, particularly in contrast to the architecture firm, where we usually worked straight through lunch at our desks.

One of the most interesting aspects of the business was its hybrid business model. The gallery's emphasis was on arts and fashion and the majority of the money from sales went back into rebuilding the communities in Mexico where the art came from. The ethos of the company was to educate and inspire, which resonated on a deep level with me and with the people who bought the artwork. I was encouraged to see a profit could be made through a non-profit approach, and the clients loved that their money was going directly back to the artists. This love of giving back to the communities where the art was being made, to the community in San Francisco where the business was operating, and to the employees was an incredible inspiring business model for me.

Thankfully, the gallery offered a significant employee discount, which meant that for the first time, I could afford to buy art. Some of the objects that came in were significantly more valuable than others. We featured tapestries, weavings, paintings, a few pieces of furniture, and a variety of clothing. I kept my eyes on the prices as things were marked down and waited patiently for my opportunity.

We got a beautiful hand-painted bar stool in one day from a fairly well known artist named Botero. I researched him and knew the stool was a valuable item. When it first arrived, the price tag on it was very high, but it was in the store for some time and didn't sell. I watched the price drop 10%, 20%, 25%, and ultimately, 40% off the ticket price. The employee discount was the best offer minus an additional 30%, and at that price it was a steal.

I called my mom and dad, told them about the bar stool and said they needed to buy it. They had a restaurant in Glen Gardner, NJ and it would be beautiful in the space.

My mom collected minor pieces of art over the years, and I knew she would love the figurative nature of Botero's work. They purchased the bar stool and I had it shipped to New Jersey. It was exciting to sell a piece of art again, especially one of such great value. It also meant a lot that my parents were on board and trusted me to make the purchase.

The Botero stool was the first personal piece of major art I researched and helped a "client" acquire outside of the few art sales I made at the gallery in New York 1997. It was an exhilarating moment for me. From then on, I started to pay more attention to the value and pricing of objects and artwork. Buying something for a fraction of its value is a real rush. It's probably one of the aspects of my job I enjoy the most today. I love to help people build a collection, especially within a wide range of budgets. Some of my clients ask me to go hunting for specific pieces or source them through various channels, and I love the thrill of the chase.

During this time, I was trying to figure out what I ultimately wanted to do for work. I was back in the grind of working seven days a week, not for the money, but because I wanted keep my footing in the art market and see what was possible. My position at the firm was taking a toll. I tried to reconcile what I was learning with the wealthy lifestyles of our clients and the entitlement of the architects I was exposed to, but to no avail. The panic attacks continued, virtually unabated, the entire time I was there, despite my attempts to manage them through deep breathing.

In yoga class one night, during a particularly stressful week at work, the instructor led us into a heart-opening pose. Right in the middle of the pose, I was overcome by an overwhelming feeling of fear; fear for my future and fear for my career path. Tears poured down my face and I was unable to control the loud, gasping sobs. Ordinarily, I am an extremely controlled and reserved person; I could not figure out what was happening to me. A few minutes passed and I realized, with crystal clear clarity, that I was lonely and unhappy. I missed my family and felt disconnected from the people in my life. After three years of adventure, it was time to go home.

PART III

A DREAM REALIZED

nine

PHILADELPHIA

THE RETURN TO THE EAST COAST WAS PERFECTLY timed to coincide with summer at the Jersey Shore. I couldn't wait to get to my parent's place on Long Beach Island. They were over the moon that I had finally decided to come home and spend some time with them. I had a few friends in the area and got a great summer job at the Loveladies Foundation for the Arts.

It was easy to fall right back into my old familiar groove, working during the day and hanging out with my parents and their friends at night. A bunch of people from high school and college were around that summer, and everyone was staring to fall into their respective career paths.

I felt the pressure to get my act together. I was 25 years old. My friends were making huge salaries, living in nice apartments in New York City, driving fancy cars, and buying grown up furniture. I was living with my parents and basically starting from scratch.

My parents were thrilled I was home and I was happy about the decision as well. For the first time in a long time, we were in agreement and it felt really great. I still wasn't sure what my career would look like, but I knew I wanted it to be in the arts.

Philadelphia, at the time, was not terribly well known for its art scene. In fact, the art community was incredibly small and insular. There were only a handful of galleries operating and most of them were not hiring. I kept sending my resume to different places and in perfect timing for the end of summer; I managed to find a job with a start-up gallery in Old City. I was quickly learning about the economic structure of the arts in Philadelphia. The pay was almost half what it would have been at a larger gallery or in New York, but I was hired to help develop the business from the ground up. I knew this opportunity would be invaluable to me down the road so it made perfect sense to me.

Immediately, I was struck by the vast differences between New York City and Philadelphia, which was considerably smaller. There is a distinctly blue-collar, working-man mentality in Philly, which really resonated with me. I'm a scrapper myself and felt way more comfortable among other hardworking, gritty people than I did hobnobbing with fancy, rich people.

My exposure to the city until that point in my life was fairly limited. I had been there a few times to eat or go shopping at Zipperheads, the punk store on South Street, but I'd never spent any real time there. Its small size made it easy to navigate on foot. I spent a good amount of time in the first few weeks just walking around and exploring the different neighborhoods. I quickly fell madly in love with the city. Everyone was friendly and welcoming. I had daily conversations with the shop owners in Old City where I was working and living, and quickly built up a small community around me.

At the gallery, I was responsible for all aspects related to business development, daily operations, and management. I helped get key functions and documents into place such as press releases and press lists. I grew the mailing list with local community members and contacts. It felt in many ways like I was opening my own gallery because the owners had daytime corporate jobs. They funded the operation and decided what art was exhibited and sold and they trusted my experience to develop business ideas that would help us grow.

Philadelphia is one of many small cities that hosts "First Friday" every month. It is a night where all of the galleries and artist co-ops stay open a few hours late, so people can come out after work to see new exhibitions and drink wine. Through these events and from being in the gallery, I met a lot of artists who were making art and involved in art-related activities around the city. It didn't take long to grow a network. For the first time ever, I started to feel like things were going to happen for me in this town. The community was buzzing with new restaurants, new buildings, and economic expansion. There was a great energy and excitement bubbling. I started to pick up extra work doing a little consulting and curating outside of the gallery with a start-up design company.

The more out on the scene I was, the more people I met. A handful of local artists turned to me for help with their resumes or websites. I started my own side business to help them grow professionally and better publicize their work. From being in New York for a year at a top gallery and spending my summers there at the best art institutions, I had a strong sense of what made someone talented in the larger marketplace and what real quality was. I spent hours working on professional artist resumes and also looking into opportunities and grants for established artists. There were several incredible MFA programs in the area that were graduating artists with very strong portfolios. I was drawn to the young, emerging, contemporary artists and started to uncover a real opportunity to help them.

At the time in Philadelphia in 2000, there were no commercial galleries dedicated exclusively to young and emerging artists. This part of the art market was becoming hot as collectors in New York, LA, and London were very interested in finding talent that had not yet exploded in the marketplace so galleries around the United States were slowly adding this as an offering to their programming. Philadelphia seemed to be behind all of this, although artist-run cooperative spaces were becoming more hip. I was meeting artists who were forming these collective spaces where an artist could join and pay a monthly fee. The artwork we sold at the gallery did not resonate with me on the same level as the artists I was working with on the side. Some of the pieces were very expensive but I couldn't quite understand why. I didn't see the value or recognize the quality in the work. I started to feel inauthentic about selling work I wouldn't hang up on my own walls. It felt like lying.

There was a time at that gallery when I sold a significant piece of art to a client and felt hollow afterwards. I was only able to focus on selling art I would purchase, which was quite limited because of my specific preference for contemporary art. I was also frustrated that my paycheck was not equivalent to the amount of energy going into the would need to find either a second job or beef up my curatorial side projects to make ends meet.

I couldn't figure out how everyone in the art world was surviving. I was barely able to make ends meet, even with a degree from a prestigious college, extensive gallery experience and my amazing summer internships. I knew I wanted to be in that world, but clearly I had to dig a little deeper to figure out how to make it happen.

I went to Barnes & Noble to see if there were any books about how to be successful in the arts. Nothing. I had to expand my scope. I was in the business section when a small blue and white book caught my attention. It was called, *The E-Myth: Why Most Small Businesses Don't Work and What to Do About It* by Michael Gerber. Something compelled me to buy it. Little did I know the content would change the course of my life and career.

My name started to pop up in the press because of a few shows I curated in other spaces for artists I met around town. The gallery owners at my job saw a potential conflict of interest between the work I was doing on the side and my work at their gallery. They wanted all of the projects I worked on to be under their gallery name, which didn't sit right with me. Their program did not represent my interests and I did not want to confuse the two. They couldn't offer me a full-time salary and I couldn't offer them an exclusive commitment. After a friendly conversation about it, we decided to part ways. I started to think I could run my own gallery.

Because of Michael Gerber's book, I realized the answer I'd been looking for was right in front of me. The people making the most money in my industry were the gallery owners and the business owners. I'd thought I didn't have enough technical or business skills to start my own business, but I wanted to transition from the worker side of the fence to the business owner side. It dawned on me I'd spent years working in galleries and running art organizations. I knew enough to get started. I just needed to put myself in the driver seat. Could I run *my own* gallery?

I was living in a tiny one-bedroom walkup apartment on 7th and Pine St., near Washington Square, in the heart of town. Within just a few blocks, I had a nightclub, a hospital, a coffee shop, a pizza parlor, and a cheesesteak shop. At the time, I was still making paintings here and there. I approached a local coffee shop owner and a restaurant owner in Old City and started curating artist exhibitions in their spaces, each month with community artists.

By juggling a handful of small consulting and art advising projects, I was just barely able to make ends meet. The Capital Grill on Broad Street was getting ready to open and they hired me to help with their art placement. A few different curating opportunities came my way too. My goal was to meet as many people and get as much exposure as possible so as to develop sales and contacts from the exhibitions I was curating and the clients I consulted for. I also wanted to work directly with a select handful of local artists to promote their work.

Pre-Internet, almost everything of significance came my way through advertisements in the paper: job opportunities, apartment vacancies, and—when I was ready to try to make it on my own—artists. I placed an ad online and one in *The Philadelphia Inquirer*. I was looking for artists and artworks for corporate consulting projects. I was interested specifically in working with professional contemporary artists who had graduate degrees. An address was provided where they could send me their slides and additional detailed information. Packets started arriving in the mail and if the slides appealed to me, I'd set up a meeting. We'd talk about their goals and what motivated them and how they worked. Getting to know the artists and understanding how they worked propelled me forward.

I was representing five local artists in the early days. They paid me a monthly consulting fee to help them find opportunities, beef up their resumes, edit their portfolios, and place their work in various collections around the city, both private and corporate. I was talking to everyone I met about art.

After a short time, it became clear I needed somewhere of my own to show the work. I took over the living room in my walk up apartment and turned it into a gallery. I went to Home Depot and bought track lighting and a few cans of white paint. I hung the art on the walls and brought anyone to the space who wanted to look at art. The bedroom became my makeshift office during the day. I put all my stuff away in closets and made the place look sterile and professional to meet with artists and clients.

Though rudimentary, it was a pretty good starter setup.

I had to be creative in how the art was displayed, but I was using all of the skills and systems collected from my past experiences and applying them to my own endeavor. It felt like I might actually be onto something big.

My first sale after quitting the gallery besides the Capital Grille project was to a cab driver on my way home from a frame shop. I was carrying one of my artist's watercolors in a huge black portfolio case. When I climbed into the back of his car, the cab driver and I started chatting. He asked me what I did and I told him I was just starting my own business as an art advisor. Turns out, he and his wife loved art. He asked if he could see what was in my case.

We pulled over on the side of the road, he stopped the meter, and we started passing 8 x 10 watercolors back and forth through the glass divider. I told him all about the artist and why his work was important. He was part of the Mural Arts program in Philadelphia, which was gaining traction and attention at the time.

The cab driver liked the traditional landscapes and asked about pricing. The paintings were $400 unframed, but he was interested in having them framed. Since I was on my way home from the frame shop, I had sample molds right in my bag, which I pulled out in the back of the cab. We started to play around with which frames looked best with which painting, and as luck would have it, the cab driver was interested in buying a few pieces.

He drove me to the makeshift gallery space in my

apartment and I invited him up to see some of the larger paintings. It felt a little weird to invite a total stranger into my apartment, but I felt safe with him and he was going to leave his cab parked illegally outside the building, so we had to hurry. He decided on two small pieces with framing and asked if I could help frame some other work he had at home for his wife.

This was my first independent sale to a regular art collector and it was close to $1,000. I had generated a sale from scratch. It was a huge moment in my career. I thought, "If I can sell art to a cab driver, then I can do this. I'm on my way!" Within the first two weeks of going solo, I generated several thousands of dollars, which was more than I had made in a month at the gallery. I have always been a spiritual and intuitive person who believes in myself. Positive moments showed up for me in those early days that told me I was on the right path, even though I was terrified to live without a salary for the first time in my life.

The sale to the cab driver was pivotal for a few reasons. I realized it was not wise to make a habit of inviting strangers into my apartment. Aside from the safety issue, it did not help me to appear professional. Even though I made my apartment look like a traditional gallery, at the end of the day, it just wasn't.

A light bulb went off. I realized that between the five artists I was representing and some of the other projects

I had going on the side, I had the makings to start my own real, legitimate gallery. Selling art out of my apartment, fun though it was, was not a sustainable arrangement. I didn't want to go and work for someone else again because I had tasted the freedom of curating and selling art on my own terms. I knew I had the skills and knowledge to pull off a gallery of my own.

Never in my wildest dreams did I think I would be a business owner. I was comfortable being an employee. But I was most definitely at a crossroads. There weren't any galleries in Philadelphia that were showing the type of work I wanted to sell, which was specifically emerging artists from Philadelphia with a graduate degree. Many of the artists in Philadelphia were either already established on their own, with galleries that had been around for ten or fifteen years, or self-taught hobbyists.

It was 2001, I was 26 years old, and I wanted to show professional artists who were my age. I wanted to represent a handful of carefully selected, academic, formally trained artists who represented the sensibilities and quality I had come to appreciate in New York. After spending thousands of hours in galleries in the city, working in one for a year and being in the marketplace, I had the confidence to identify a good artist or one who had potential.

One of my early favorite painters is the American abstract artist, Jean-Michel Basquiat. I learned about him during an "art in the dark" art history class in college.

His style of painting opened up the art world for me. I was drawn to his penchant for raw, graffiti-like mark making; street art and symbology combined with cultural black expression. I wanted to base my program around artists who fit the same aesthetic.

One of my requirements is that each artist I work with have a dramatically individualized process of painting or art making that makes their work stand out. The Pennsylvania Academy of Fine Arts is among one of the most highly regarded art schools in the city, but most of the graduates at the time were focusing on traditional portraiture or landscape painting. A lot of the work coming out of there all looked the same to me and I was after something edgier and more distinct.

Through the ads I placed online and in the paper, I was able to find a handful of Philadelphia artists who embodied what I was looking for. Once the aesthetic was established, referrals started to pour in. Word of mouth and a growing excitement led to a healthy stable of about 15 artists, all of whom had distinctive styles and unique work. I called my first exhibition "Young & Fun" because I felt it represented the program and the type of gallery I was going to operate.

I felt we were on the same page and in the same boat together. As they developed professionally, so would I. It was a true partnership and their successes would lead invariably toward mine and mine back to theirs. With my

stable in place and my trademark pile of determination,
I was ready to make a real go of it in the Philadelphia
gallery scene.

t e n

THE GALLERY

AFTER BEING IN THE CITY FOR ABOUT SIX MONTHS, Philadelphia had gotten under my skin. I felt connected to it in a way I never did in New York, San Francisco, or Taipei. Although I appreciated those cities for their unique beauty, size, and character, the Philly vibe was just right for me. It was large enough to have many vibrant flavors and opportunities, but small enough to feel like a real community. Each neighborhood had its own distinct character.

I ran or walked everywhere in the first few months of living there. I was scoping out a neighborhood for my future gallery and it was fascinating to see which parts of the city were developing and which sections were neglected. Washington Square was an area that fell into the latter category. It was surprising that a neighborhood smack dab in the middle of the city fell into such a state of disrepair. There were drug addicts and homeless people loitering in the park and the buildings were largely run down, but it was central to everything.

Most of the galleries back then were closer to Old City, but I wanted to be separate from the pack. There weren't too many other commercial businesses on the 700 block of Washington Square because it was primarily residential, but I figured, I could be a pioneer. Plus, leases in some of the other, more established sections of town were way out of my price range. My plan was to use my marketing skills to draw people to me, instead of planting myself in the middle of the competition.

Everything fell into place quite fortuitously and very quickly. One day, I was getting coffee at 7th and Walnut Street and noticed an "office for rent" sign on a dirty white dilapidated building. There were two boarded up, filthy windows so I couldn't see inside. The rental space was on the ground floor of a brownstone in the middle of the block, just a stone's throw away from Washington Square. I called the landlord to arrange for a walk through.

The place was filled to the rafters with old furniture and memorabilia. It smelled dusty and was in disrepair, but I was intrigued. The woman who owned the building had just passed away a year or so earlier and she was a patron of the arts and music in Philadelphia. Her son was a teacher and lived in Colorado and was trying to rent the space, but he didn't want to rent it to just anyone. I was told that several other people were also interested. I really liked the space and felt the potential, so I was worried about a bidding war. There was an attorney, a dentist, and even a restaurateur all vying for it at the same time as I was.

As luck would have it again, the son wanted a tenant who would be minimally invasive. A gallery appealed to him because it would honor his mother's love of art. He grew up in the building and was attached to it. His parents used the ground floor and the basement for their office and the rest of the brownstone was their residence. Art had covered the walls and the hallways, salon style like the Barnes Collection. My intention to turn the space into a gallery was *the* deciding factor and the son took my bid over everyone else's. It was meant to be. I felt like the woman who had owned the building was smiling on me from the grave.

Later on, once I was in the space, I could actually feel her presence in the building. Her husband had passed away five years before she did, and she used to sit in the window, looking out at Washington Square, for hours every single day. She was something of a legend in the neighborhood and once I moved in, people started to stop by and tell me stories about her. Without knowing it, I set up my desk right where she used to sit. This unnerved one of the neighbors who came in one day and said, "Oh, you remind us of old Mrs. Hanby. She used to sit just where you are sitting now and look out at the park and watch all of the comings and goings." Her energy was all around the space, and it was a very comforting, positive energy.

I signed a one-year lease and negotiated the use of the basement as part of the package which they agreed to happily. The family had been in restaurant equipment sales and set up the basement as a kitchen and entertainment space with a big, long, medieval, wooden dining room table and chairs. There was a bathroom and a shower and windows at the base of the building, so a little bit of natural light came through. There was also decent floor lighting and plenty of room. My plan was to use it as storage for the gallery where it was safe and dry. When I was officially in the building, there was another trip to Home Depot for white paint and track lights and I quickly got to work. I was ready to clean it up and make it my own.

I was 26 years old and full of hope for the future. Like most endeavors, there were a few obstacles to deal with fresh out of the gate. The first problem was it very hard to get people to take me seriously. I have always looked very young for my age, which is not something that one typically associates with a problem, but when I was 26, I looked like I was still in high school.

People came right out and said, "You look way too young to own a gallery. What could you possibly know about emerging artists? Do you having business partners who are behind the scenes running things for you?" I was amazed by how brash and forthright people are with their every thought. Most of my early conversations with people started this way, and I found myself in the uncomfortable position of having to defend my experience and my resume at every turn.

Plus, even though I felt like I had met a lot of people during the first few months in town, I hadn't established a name or a reputation for myself. I wasn't a local on the scene and most of the people in the art world had no clue who I was or what I was trying to do. To make matters even worse, I was in a double bind because the stable of artists I represented were also completely unknown. No one knew if the artists or I would even be around in the next year, let alone five years. Some of the conversations in those early days were infuriating, but they only gave me more fuel to thrive and succeed.

I took care of a sick aunt in high school one summer, and when she passed away she left me a small inheritance. Between the money from her and some money I had saved up, I had about $30,000. My rent was $1,000 and my monthly overhead was around $3,000. I figured I had enough money to last for about ten months. In hindsight, the naivety of this assumption is staggering. I hadn't researched start-up costs or factored in marketing dollars and a whole host of additional expenses that popped up. I had to put down a $500 deposit to set up a commercial utility account. I remember my first electric bill was close to $500, and I had a panic attack. There were so many major expenses I hadn't anticipated and my ten-month runway quickly shriveled to about six.

Nevertheless, the Bridgette Mayer Gallery opened in the summer of 2001. I previewed for a few weeks in May and opened officially on June 1st. When I burned through several months' worth of savings just to get open, I started to worry about bringing in enough money to make ends meet.

I was learning constantly. An immediate lesson was that Philadelphia empties out during the summer months. When the kids get out of school, most of the people with the means to buy art take off for the beach, just as my own family did for summers at the Jersey Shore. I had a big grand opening, and I sold one or two pieces during the opening, which helped me to recoup some of the launch costs. The arts editor of *The Philadelphia Inquirer* wrote a review of my first group show, which helped to pique the public's interest. In mid-July, things got eerily quiet, and they stayed that way for the next few months. This was new to me; I started to realize there are cycles of business.

By late August, I started to freak out. Thoughts such as, "Oh god, what have I done? I'm never going to make it. This is way harder than I imagined it would ever be!" started to march through my head. I began the fall season with a group show and an opening to launch the work the first week of September. Few people came out because almost everyone was still at the beach for the last week of summer. Nothing sold. Things were not looking good.

My primary goal was to make it through the first year so I wouldn't have to default on the lease, something I had never done before. My own expenses were not a concern and the business had to come first. I began to make shifts in my spending. All of my meals were prepared at home and I put a moratorium on coffee shops and restaurants. Time to bootstrap.

The lean philosophy of business became one of my core financial principles over the years. All of the profit was funneled back into the gallery, which is a behavior practiced by many entrepreneurs. Instead of spending money on myself, I reinvested in advertising or marketing to boost awareness for the artists. All of my efforts went into surviving.

I was operating from sheer will and determination during the first year, with the intention of putting everything I had into the monthly exhibitions. I focused on meeting as many people as I could in the community and being as open and accessible as possible. My emphasis was solely on putting together an unbeatable program that would get noticed. If that meant 12- or 15-hour days, so be it.

Whenever anyone asked me how things were going, I lied and said they couldn't be better. No one wants to buy from a struggling business, especially in the art world. There was nothing to do but put on a happy face and pretend I wasn't watching my sales and my savings dwindle. To the public, my family, and my friends, I downplayed my fears, determined to push through and see the other side of success. There was too much at stake to give in to doubt, or reality.

My desk was set up at the front of the building in front of two huge windows that stretched almost from the floor to the ceiling. Like an actor on a stage, I sat there most days and into the night on my laptop on full view to anyone walking by. There wasn't any extra cash for an assistant and I was doing all of the work myself: answering the phones during the day, sending out mailings, writing press releases, updating my website, writing client letters, making appointments, hanging shows, moving and wrapping art to sell, patching and painting the walls, and cleaning the space in between my exhibitions. Looking back, I must have appeared slightly manic to anyone passing by. Either that or exhausted from trying so hard.

One night, I was in the gallery, working at my desk as usual when I heard tapping on the window. A nicely dressed older gentleman was standing there motioning to come in. He lived in the neighborhood and liked to eat dinner at a restaurant near Washington Square. He told me he had noticed me in there working at all hours and would love to come in and take a closer look at the show. I often left the lights on so people could see the art from the street. After midnight, I turned the lights off because

I didn't want people seeing me in there working, but the glow of my laptop was constant.

The man had been looking at the art through the windows for a few weeks and was intrigued. I was working anyway, so I invited him in and gave him a tour of the show. We had a lovely conversation. He had purchased some small works of art in the past, but nothing larger than 30 x 30. The paintings I was exhibiting were huge. He loved the artist's work and dreamed of having one of the large paintings in his living room. I followed up and sent him the artist's information the next day. A week later, he came back in during regular business hours and bought his first major contemporary painting for $4,000. It was a huge sale for me and a big step for him. He made his first significant art acquisition at my gallery and he's been a client and friend ever since.

With a client list of over five hundred collectors, I am fortunate to have about fifty private clients, just like him, who I adore working with; people I've been collaborating with and helping to buy art for the last 16 years. Most of them buy exclusively from me. Their collections have expanded into international art and museum-level artists, and I have been their private advisor each step of the way. Their loyalty and faith in my advice is a large part of why I've been able to build a successful business. This started early on because I always spent hours talking to each of the visitors who came through the gallery. Developing the relationships over the years and getting to know what people like and what they get excited about has unquestionably been one of the most rewarding and most fun parts of my work.

But success did not come overnight by any stretch. Philadelphia remained largely empty long after Labor Day. A handful of curious potential clients trickled through the gallery in those first few months but aside from my one big sale, there was a lot of hustle and very little bustle.

On the morning of 9/11, I was working with a wealthy furniture maker I had met at a networking event. He was interested in possibly buying some pieces for a recently acquired condominium. We were deep in conversation and carefully studying one or two larger paintings when the gallery phone started ringing. Whenever I was with a client, I focused exclusively on them and never interrupted the meeting for things like phone calls. The phone kept ringing and ringing, and it went unanswered.

Washington Square usually got busy around noon when people headed out for lunch. On that day, I noticed a lot more people outside and on the sidewalks, but it didn't occur to me to go outside and find out what was happening.

The man I was working with was interested in seeing how both of the pieces he was interested in looked in his new space. I made the necessary arrangements to get the work over to his condo and remained focused on my client. I met him at his place and he wound up buying one of the pieces. At last, a sale!

He asked me if I had spoken to anyone besides him all day, which I thought was weird. I said, "No, you're it so far. I have been working on getting this work over to you. Why do you ask?" He chose not to tell me what was going on in New York and Washington. I think he must have felt the news was too severe for him to be the one to deliver it to me.

When I got back to the gallery later that afternoon, the phone was still ringing off the hook. I ran to grab it and it was my mom. She asked me if I had seen the news and I told her I'd been with a client and asked why she sounded so frantic. She yelled, "Bridgette, you've got to get out of there! Your neighborhood is under a bomb scare. Get to a TV! There was a terrorist attack in New York. Everyone is freaking out." I told her I was fine and would call her later, and then I got the hell out of there.

I ran all the way home, turned on the TV, and watched in horror with the rest of the world the same scene replaying over and over of the planes hitting the World Trade Center and the twin towers falling. Everything came to a standstill. No one was going out and no one was coming into the gallery. The whole country burrowed down and waited for answers.

At the end of the month, one of the artists in the group show came by. I talked him into buying a print he had been admiring. That sale and the one I made on 9/11 was all the income I had for the month. It was enough to cover the phone bill and the rent. I decided there was nothing I could do except to be positive and carry on.

I kept putting in the hours and told myself to embrace the quiet time and make the most of it. Every month, I geared up for a new opening. Every month, nothing sold. After the 9/11 attacks, people were making buying decisions based on fear. I started to learn about the psychology behind how, why, and where people spend money. The only thing to do was put myself out there and try to get as much exposure as possible. I went to every networking event on the calendar and kept myself busy.

Six months after opening and stretching every dollar, I had still only sold five paintings. There was only one thing left for me to give up, which was my apartment. I decided the best thing to do was get rid of it, save myself the monthly expense of rent, and move into the basement of the gallery. It had running water, a shower, and kitchen. What more did I need?

The decision had been made, but I decided to keep it under wraps. If some of the wealthy people I was trying to cultivate as clients knew I was living in the basement, they would never want to buy art from me. And forget about telling my parents. I would show them next time they came to visit.

I spent a weekend bleaching the basement from end to end and top to bottom. It was riddled with mold and cockroaches that had to be dealt with. The space was pretty large, about 1500 square feet, and it took three straight days to get rid of the mold that covered the walls and the beams in the ceilings. I was lightheaded from the effort and may have passed out in there a few times from the fumes.

A little dirty work didn't scare me. I just had to roll up my sleeves and get it done. The work ethic came from all those years of working on the farm with my dad. I had spent weekends mucking horse dung out of barns and went home at the end of the day covered in the stuff. Comparatively, bleaching and scrubbing the basement was nothing. Once the place had been cleaned and aired out, I moved in with a mattress, one suitcase of clothes, and some toiletries. So began my adventures of living in secret in the basement.

The good news was now I could spend even more time working! In the mornings after a shower, I'd head upstairs with a cup of coffee and get cracking. The doors were open every day of the week; there was zero downtime. It didn't matter to me, though. There wasn't any money to do anything else anyway. My diet became incredibly Spartan and I survived off cans of soup and Ramen. I'd been down this road before, and I knew how to make almost nothing stretch into something. I kept believing in what was possible and held onto my dream to make it work.

Looking back, opening an art gallery is probably one

of the most challenging business choices I could have made. In many ways, it's a lot like opening a restaurant. I wasn't getting a whole lot of support in the early days, but the artists were in my corner cheering me on faithfully.

The museums and wealthy people who bought art in Philadelphia, however, were less welcoming and appreciative of my hard work. No one came to my openings, even out of curiosity. My invitations went unacknowledged. The feeling of rejection was too overwhelming to ignore, but in many ways, it only inspired me to make my gallery a success all the more.

I decided to press on and build my business and program the way I wanted to. If the art patrons of Philadelphia weren't interested in the level of quality I was bringing to the scene, it was their loss and not mine. Years later, I learned that most people at the time simply were not buying art in Philadelphia. They went to Europe, New York, or California instead, which was more of a snub to the city than it was to me. I just couldn't understand why they wouldn't want to contribute to the cultural vibrancy of their own town.

My client list from the first eight to ten years is made up of people who were starting to collect for the first time. Most of them didn't have much money, but they had an appreciation for the type of work I was selling. They got it, and as a result, many of them got a hold of some amazing work at a great price.

The business was built purely from my own sweat equity. I didn't come onto the scene with a business partner, a list of patrons, or a family that was going to give me contacts. The people who wandered in randomly off the street are responsible for creating the reputation of the gallery. We would have great interactions born out of natural inquiry. I told them all about the artists and how they worked and what was inspiring to them. If the work resonated, those who were interested would buy a piece, or I would follow up constantly and talk them through the process until they finally felt comfortable spending money.

This is one of my favorite characteristics about the gallery. It was a great democratization of art. You don't have to be rich and live in a penthouse to buy something of value that you love. I could not relate to people who bought art for decoration or because someone else told them to. It's hard to make a real connection with people like that.

I knew going in, the art market tends to be very superficial. I'd seen my fair share of it in New York and even Philadelphia. But I was confident I could cultivate a group of people who were actually interested in the art and the artists. The best place to start was with the people who were interested enough to cross the threshold. I decided to focus on them instead of worry about the people who, for whatever reason, never came by.

When I shifted my concentration to the people right in

front of me, the business started to thrive and my client list grew. My intention was to give everyone who came in a great experience. I wanted the artists to get to know the people who were buying their art and share in the relationship. Likewise, I wanted the clients to know the artists. When it was time for an installation, the artist came with me and told the story about how and why the piece was made. This level of personal connection with the artists allowed the clients to understand how significantly they were contributing to our community, to the artists, and to my business.

The clients became invested beyond the dollar value of the art on the walls. Their added takeaway was getting to live with a beautiful piece of art they had picked out themselves and that had special meaning for them. They spent their hard-earned money bringing art into their homes.

Together, the early clients, the artists, and I were all growing together through an incredible, authentic, and organic support process. As I became exposed to more and more artists, I started to realize I was able to offer them something that hadn't existed before—genuine support. Five years into owning the gallery, it hit me: this was working. I was doing it! I was developing a stable of artists and together we were building a community.

e l e v e n

EVOLUTION

ON ONE OR TWO OCCASIONS, ONE OF MY ARTISTS asked me to say a few words at the beginning of their art opening. It's not an unusual request, but despite my success with the gallery and the aggressive networking I had embarked on to launch it, my shyness was still with me. On some level, I naïvely assumed that my business didn't require speaking in front of large groups. I was the master of my destiny and, therefore, I didn't have to do anything that made me uncomfortable.

I tried to speak at one of the openings on behalf of my artist but it was a colossal failure. The experience was a reminder to avoid any situation that might require being in the spotlight; an impractical path for someone who is trying to make a name for herself.

Some time into the second year of the gallery being

open, advertising in art magazines became one of my marketing priorities. I committed to an ad a month in one of the better-known publications and planned to purchase two covers. It was important to have my name splashed all over town, in magazines and newspapers that potential clients were likely to read, so when they thought about galleries, they'd think about me. I knew enough about marketing to understand the power of being a part of the collective subconscious.

Due to the ad campaign, people were starting to see my name more and more. Requests to speak to groups or be on panels started to come in, but I said no to every inquiry, always making up a hasty excuse to get out of it. The University of Pennsylvania invited me to speak and Bucknell asked me to come back to campus to talk about my experience of being a gallery owner. Again, I said no.

A huge part of marketing is participating in just the types of events I was being invited to. I knew I was shooting myself in the foot and my attitude toward public speaking had to change. For the sake of the gallery's success and to better promote my artists, it was becoming increasing necessary to get out of my own way and over my fear of public speaking once and for all.

I started reading about my problem and found an amazing book called *Feel the Fear and Do it Anyway* by Susan Jeffers. In it, she talks about the relationship between fear and anxiety. The panic attacks I had experienced for years were still occurring. My heart would start to pound out of my chest and my face went beet red. Sometimes they would get so bad, I felt like I might pass out. Jeffers solution was to make a commitment to dealing with it. Push past it until you are ready to accept the fear as a reality, but something that can be overcome. Acknowledge, accept, breathe, deal, repeat.

The day I finished the book, I made the commitment. I would say yes to the next ten things I was asked to do, no matter what they were. The very next day, the phone rang. It was a producer from CNN. She said they had seen an article about me in the Bucknell alumni magazine. I spoke with her briefly about my background and she said she was interested in doing a profile on me.

She was working on a new show featuring Anderson Cooper called, "On The Rise." I thought someone was prank calling me. She went on to say they wanted to send a camera crew to the gallery in Philadelphia to shadow me for a day. Anderson Cooper would introduce the edited interview on national TV when it aired.

Once I got over the disbelief and scheduled a date with her, I sat at my desk stunned. It was only one day since I had committed to stop saying "no" and the first thing to show up was Anderson Cooper and CNN? I looked up and said, "You have got to be kidding me." The commitment had been made, and I had to say yes.

It was decided they would come to Philadelphia on

the day of a new opening so they could see everything that went into the preparations, meet the artists, and talk to a few clients. They wanted to shadow me and see an entire "day in the life" of a young gallery owner. This was exposure on a whole new level; a national TV level.

There was only a two-week time period between the CNN producer's phone call to the film crew's arrival. Within that short window, things started to snowball. I was asked to be on an emerging artist panel in Philadelphia and said yes. Bucknell caught wind of the CNN interview and asked if I would speak at parent's weekend about how I ran my business. I said yes. The art history department wanted me to speak to one of the classes about what it was like working with artists. Again, yes. Someone else heard I was going to be on campus and asked if I would participate in a symposium on running a creative art business. Yes! Then I got a call from the career development center. Could I organize and deliver a presentation about being a leader within the art industry? Um, yes.

Within days of reading Jeffers' book, CNN was booked, I'd committed to being on the panel in Philadelphia, and Bucknell had me scheduled for four separate engagements over three days. This saying yes stuff had taken on a life of its own. I decided to hire someone to get some coaching on how to navigate my new world of massive exposure. I found someone who worked with a lot of famous actors to get them comfortable in their roles through the "Alexander Technique." I spent quite a bit of time preparing my talks and practicing what to say and how to say it.

The day of the CNN shoot, I was a nervous wreck. I did not sleep the night before. I didn't want to look like a sweaty, red-faced wreck on national TV. Even though they were there all the day, the camera guys assured me all of the footage would be edited down into a one-minute segment, which was a lot easier to stomach than a whole hour about me. I had an incredible afternoon. We started in the gallery and then I took them to a meeting with a corporate client who did not mind having CNN in tow with me. Next we went to an artist's studio for a meeting and then they interviewed me for an hour. They filmed the opening and got sound bites from the people who came out for the show.

I sent out a press release to the art community about the show, which resulted in a few more local articles. New faces started to come into the gallery as a result of the Anderson Cooper piece. People finally figured if I was good enough for CNN, then maybe they should come and see for themselves what was happening at the gallery. Phone inquiries and emails from outside of Philadelphia began pouring in. I had been so primarily focused on Philadelphia in the first few years, I hadn't considered the impact national exposure would have for the gallery.

CNN received such a positive outpouring of praise on their website about the clip, I was invited to New York to participate in a panel with four other successful business people. I was asked to curate a show at their headquarters in the Time Warner building. All of the positive press and the activities that followed, as a result, were reason enough to keep on saying yes. As much as I didn't want to admit it to myself, marketing, publicity, and speaking engagements are a huge part of the art business. I still feel shy and nervous whenever it's time to be in the spotlight, but I've learned how to keep the end goal in mind and deal with the fear.

The gallery was finally starting to turn a profit. My stable of artists was developing nicely. They were enjoying their own successes and a fair share of notoriety within the community. Commissioned projects and corporate projects were coming to fruition. The program and the core group of artists I represented were my main focus.

In 2007, just before the market crashed, I was given the opportunity to buy the building where the gallery was housed. The fortuitous nature that surrounded my securing the lease in the first place stayed with me. I was in the right place at the right time.

Over the years, I took care of the building as if it was my own. The son who owned the building in Colorado and I had built up a relationship. The floors, hallways, and stairs were always swept clean and the windows were crystal clear. I didn't ask for money; I just wanted to be a great tenant so he would keep me in the building. He knew I loved the space and was very appreciative of how well I took care of it. When he decided to sell, he told me about his plans months before he even spoke to a real estate agent. He wanted to give me an opportunity to get my ducks in a row, which by that point, I was able to do.

When I signed the original lease for the space, the real estate agent suggested we add a clause into my lease, "the right of first refusal," to be able to make the first offer to purchase the building should the owner ever want to sell it. Boy, was I glad this was in my lease. I did have the first opportunity to make an offer on the building, which was quickly rejected. One of my neighbors, who owned several properties on the block, made an offer immediately after mine, and his was accepted.

A million dollars was a lot of money for me, but I knew this was a defining moment for me professionally and personally. I was able to counter, match the accepted offer, and purchase the building. I had been preparing for this moment for several months, ever since the owner gave me a heads up that he was selling the building. I worked hard to make it a reality. Ever since my business started to take off, I had dreamed of buying the building. There were so many things I wanted to do with the space to make it better. I was to be an official property owner in Philadelphia, on the beautiful and still-developing Washington Square.

Two years after buying the building, I realized a long-time dream of renovating the space. I wanted it to be a world-class gallery that rivaled some of the best in New York City. By working with a prominent Philadelphia architect and having a vision in mind, we transformed the gallery into easily one of the best spaces in Philadelphia. The public response when I re-opened was tremendous, and the artists were so excited to be able to show in a state-of-the-art exhibition space.

The more people I met, the more I started to understand how large the artist community was in Philadelphia. I get hundreds of emails a year from artists in Philadelphia and around the country looking for gallery representation and exhibition opportunities. One question kept popping up for me: How could I help more artists with exhibitions and sell their work without compromising the integrity of my program? Some of the new artists I met were appropriate to include in corporate presentations or curated shows outside of the gallery, but that was just a select few.

At the same time, I was starting to learn about the vast non-profit world in Philadelphia. I wanted to figure out some way to get exposure for community artists while also contributing to the non-profits. How could I combine the two? I kept thinking back to my days in San Francisco working at the gallery that contributed to multiple communities. My pockets weren't yet deep enough to write checks and hand money over. There had to be some other way. It was like trying to figure out a big city-wide puzzle to tie it all together.

I came up with a solution that was both fun and wildly successful. In 2008, the gallery hosted the first annual benefit art show for 100 artists from the community. All of the artists received a donated 10 x 10-inch clay board panel and were given the freedom to make an original piece of art that reflected their studio work. The money earned was divided between a select non-profit, the gallery to cover expenses, and the artists. It was a triple-header.

The first year, we worked with an organization called "Back on My Feet," which supported the homeless population in Philadelphia and taught them skills so they could get jobs. The organization was important to me because I had witnessed the homeless problem right outside the windows of the gallery in Washington Square. The woman who ran the non-profit was an avid runner, and its supporters largely were too, so there was synergy there as well.

The first year, we raised several thousand dollars from art sales. The media came out, I presented the non-profit with a big check, and we all got a lot of great publicity out the event. It was a great time to partner with the non-profit, and within that same year they had attracted a few large corporate sponsors. Nike donated close to $40,000 and one of the big banks made a sizeable contribution too. The non-profit almost had more money than they knew what to do with.

My goal was to work with organizations that were really desperate for funding and where it would make a difference. I didn't want to be just another name on a list of donors; I wanted to make a real impact on the community in a significant way, as did the artists who were participating. I found an organization administered through the city of Philadelphia called Ready Willing and Able (RWA), also known as the Men in Blue. The mission was to help men coming out of the prison system get set up with housing, stay drug and alcohol-free, secure jobs, and matriculate back into the civilian population. Most of the work they were doing was cleaning up the streets and different areas of the city. After meeting the program director, I committed to fundraising for RWA for two years, and again, the community came out to support the initiative.

After an incredibly powerful partnership over my two-year commitment, it was time to find my next non-profit to partner with. I started to look for people and organizations in the arts that needed financial support. I found a young non-profit called BalletX through a colleague and friend who was involved. I went to see one of their performances and was struck by the raw energy and talent of their choreography. The program felt like a perfect match for the artists I was working with. Better yet, BalletX was hungry and looking for fresh funding for programs, to pay choreographers, buy shoes, and everything else that would allow them to perform.

I wanted to help even more artists get exposure through

the BalletX benefit and accepted 300 artists into the fund-raising show. Even though we doubled in size, we still had to turn people away, which was staggering to me. The show stayed up for two months the first year, largely because of the amount of work it took to organize. My staff was about ready to kill me, but all in all we raised $27,000 for BalletX and the response was tremendous.

Some pretty cool things have happened as a result of the benefit shows. The impact they have had the artists' careers with new sales and client opportunities, on the organizations that were fundraised for, and the arts culture in Philadelphia has been incredibly fulfilling. The whole idea of using art as a way to contribute to the community was born back in San Francisco when I worked for the Mexican art gallery. The gallery owner there inspired me to see what was possible and showed me how to thank the community for their support by giving back to it.

Aside from organizing the community benefit shows for the past seven years, I've been exploring the idea of creating a foundation to award women and artists with money to support various projects including college grants. The concept is based on the Make-A-Wish Foundation model, but the cash would go toward a specific artist to fund a specific piece, residency, project, or experience and/or young disadvantaged women who don't have assistance with college expenses.

I've always been attracted to the idea of helping artists

and women who need assistance find the money to make the art they want to make. I know what having a "leg up" means because of my supportive adoptive parents. I especially value the impact that a college education has had on my life. Within my gallery program over the past sixteen years, I have been able to help my artists actualize so many of their dreams through sales and funding. Over time, I've held fundraisers to support a specific artist or group of artists and they have always been favorably received. This has opened doors for so many incredibly talented artists within the wonderful city of Philadelphia.

The gallery has been the vehicle through which I've been able to develop as a person. It has taught me how to integrate art and community. I cherish the relationships I've developed with the artists and collectors throughout the city, many of who were by my side since the very early days of struggle. We've all grown up together.

My mission has always been to create an amazing experience, whether it's for the artists, the clients, or the community. Selling art is important in my business, but life-long relationships transcend sales in terms of value and returns. A business is a part of the lifecycle of a community. The deeper into the public art space I travel, the more I understand how it all ties together. When people are able to get out of their homes and experience art outside, within their city, it takes on a new meaning.

The next evolution of my mission is going to be working

with younger people, and women in particular, who may feel intimidated by trying to develop a career in the arts. I want to share what I have learned and overcome so that others are inspired to follow their dreams. How should you get started? By first listening to that inner voice and what it is telling you. By never giving up and never surrendering to fear. Your unique contribution to the world at large lies within. Let it out. Live it.

CONCLUSION

I'VE BEEN SCARED FOR MOST OF MY LIFE. AS A small girl when my mother starved, beat, and abandoned me. As a teenager trying to balance the social pressures of high school with family and farm responsibilities. As a young college student navigating new found freedom. As a poor college graduate in New York City. As an adventurer in Taiwan. As an early career professional in San Francisco faced with overwhelming wealth and entitlement. As a hungry entrepreneur struggling to make a name for herself in the art community of Philadelphia.

I've had a few companions on this journey, not all of them easy travel buddies: fear, determination, anxiety, intuition, doubt, and always dreams—big, big dreams. I'm lucky to have always known, on some level, that if I don't move forward and step into the fear of the unknown,

I'm not living fully or authentically. Beyond money, art, or my business, my life is about giving back to the planet; it's about using my talents and not wasting them.

Mine is not a linear path from point A to Point B; it's a continual evolution. I am always asking, where can I give back? How can I repay the tremendous good fortune I've been lucky enough to receive, nurture, and harvest? What can I give to women and children in communities that need help? How can I use my own experience as a motivational tool for others? What legacy do I want to leave behind?

The art world is often associated with money, power, and privilege. There is a vast divide between the haves (the buyers) and the have-nots (the artists). The dichotomy is not lost on me. It has always been my goal to create a bridge between those who create and those who appreciate the arts, in all of its manifestations. I've been greatly rewarded by the industry as a result of my vision and the work and sacrifice I've put in to achieve it. I've never been driven by the trappings of art world associations; I'm motivated by the bigger picture. What impact can I have on those around me?

Where there is life, there is hope. Everyone faces struggles and challenges, doubts, and fear—some certainly more severely than others. But everyone has skills and dreams. Listen to the voice inside of you, not those around you. To this day, people tell me I'm crazy, or what I want to do cannot be done. Who knows what my life would be like if I had listened to this uninvited peanut gallery.

Do not be dissuaded from your path. Don't let anyone tell you, "You can't." This is your journey. This is your life. What is it you want to do? What is your vision? There's a place for everyone and we all have something unique to contribute. We all have special gifts we are born with and if you keep looking, you'll find it. Follow your intuition because it will lead, invariably, to your true north.

LOOKING FORWARD

For of those to whom much is given, much is required.
– JOHN FITZGERALD KENNEDY

My goal is to empower artists globally to step into their personal and creative power. I'm embarking on several dream projects that will help me in that pursuit.

The channels through which I mentor, inspire, and motivate artists are growing. I'm conducting one-on-one and group coaching, speaking events and workshops, and launching an online learning network called ART MBA. Artists and gallery owners who get involved in these events will benefit from my sixteen years of insight and experience in building a multimillion dollar career from scratch. I've also been fortunate to receive incredible coaching during my own journey and will include that knowledge so that each participant has the opportunity to learn from those experiences just as I did.

At the same time, I'm working on a legacy project called the Art Cure Foundation. In living from the heart of myself and giving what I have been given (as one of my favorite female mentors on the planet, Oprah Winfrey, has discussed), I want to enable young creative women to think big and support them with funding for their dream projects. The Foundation will bring together several things I love: philanthropy, empowerment of young women and artists, and the diverse tribe of people in my life who want to make the world a better place. To connect with these ventures, visit my website.

My next book is a guidebook about the business of growing a successful art gallery. It is a manual for art dealers and gallery owners—and yes, motivated artists too—whether they are just starting out or maybe already have a gallery in need of growth ideas. I'll be sharing the techniques that have allowed me to grow my business continually over the years. Readers will learn the practical application of lessons that I learned—sometimes the hard way—and they will be able to use those lessons to follow their own dreams.

Updates on these projects will be made regularly

at www.bridgettemayer.com and on my business websites www.bridgettemayergallery.com and www. bridgettemayerartadvisors.com.

ACKNOWLEDGMENTS

THE JOURNEY OF A THOUSAND MILES BEGINS WITH one step. I have many people who have been a very important part of my life, and I am not able to put on one page all of the people who have touched my life and made positive contributions to bring me to this place. It is very humbling for me to acknowledge all of you, including the folks I have not listed by name (you know who you are); you have been an important part of my life. I love you all dearly.

Considering the nuts and bolts of getting this book into place, I would like to say thank you to a few specific individuals. Without their contributions and support, this book would not have been written.

To my loving husband, Tariq Johnson, who kept pushing me to tell my story to the world and to make an impact...I finally believe you! Thanks and love to my mom, Elaine Mayer, who told me many years ago that I had a book to write, and to my dad, Russ Mayer, for details of stories. Thank you to Barry Taylor and Luke Taylor who started me on my writing journey and gave me the confidence to begin. And to the folks at Lioncrest Publishing, including Doug Watson, Kathryn Songster, Julie Stubblefield, Holly Foreman, and most especially to my favorite editor Brooke White. You are amazing Brooke.

Thank you to my special army of dear friends who were by my side with advice and feedback regarding the various mechanics: Rebecca Rutstein, Patrick Hardy, Stephen Dahlan, John Wind, Eileen Neff, Mary Smull, Frank Destra, Alex Fluker, Julie Goldstein, Blaise Niosi, Paul Oberst, Ralph Citino, Lawrence Taylor, Tom Sadler, and Garry Pezzano, as well as photographers Ben Weldon and Mark Tesi. Thank you to my mentors Joe Weldon, Cindy Rold, Craig Bradshaw, and Jake Ducey. Your positivity and light shined brightly for me during my process. With love and thanks to one of my first mentors, Ruthann Niosi, who saw my potential and helped me in so many ways. To my oldest brother Chris Mayer who has always been one of my mentors, heroes, and inspirations, and to my spiritual gurus Alysson Mayer and Louis Delmar. Thank you Seth Godin for your feedback on my cover and book marketing; your call was a delight and invaluable for me. Thank you to Michael Gerber for not only writing my book foreword, which is an honor, but also for writing the book *The E-Myth*, which set me on my path to starting my gallery business. Thank you Luz Delia Gerber for your work in coordinating all the details and for your sunshine. Thank you to Alicia Puig for your help in so many ways. Thank you to all my friends at Bucknell U, including Neil Anderson, MaryAnn Stanton, and Gigi Marino. You are all special to me. Thank you to one of the giants in my life whose passion for excellence continues to fuel me and bring me motivation and inspiration, Tony Robbins. A BIG thank you and shout out to all of my gallery artists who have given me purpose and who continue to bring creativity and fun into my life, and to my clients who have brought art into their lives and who have created and fueled many dreams. Thank you to my dear Philadelphia community. I love you. Thank you to the special group of artists who came out for my first talk and workshop, "The Art Cure Workshop 001." You all rock. And lastly, with big love, thank you all my dear siblings and family, including my new family, the Johnson and Darwish family, for giving me the space to be in your life and for sharing this life and journey with me. I LOVE YOU ALL!

ABOUT THE AUTHOR

 BRIDGETTE MAYER
is an art dealer in
Philadelphia, PA.
She opened Bridgette
Mayer Gallery on
Philadelphia's historic
Washington Square in
2001. She represents
artists from Philadelphia, New York, Los Angeles and
around the world, specializing in contemporary painting,
sculpture and photography. The gallery also deals in sec-
ondary market artwork sales and private and corporate
consulting. Her gallery produces ten regularly rotating

exhibitions a year as well as publications on major exhibitions. Gallery artists have won many prestigious awards including the Pew Fellowship in the Arts, Guggenheim Grants, Pollock-Krasner Foundation Awards, the Miami University Young Painters Competition and the Pennsylvania Council for the Arts Grant.

Bridgette Mayer Gallery has been featured on CNN's Anderson Cooper 360 as a small business "On The Rise" and was recognized as a recommended Philadelphia arts destination in The New York Times Magazine. In 2013 Mayer was awarded with the Philadelphia Business Journal 40 Under 40 Award. In 2013, 2014 & 2015 Mayer was named one of the top 500 Galleries in the world by Blouin ArtInfo, and was also interviewed and featured in the Tory Burch Foundation's "Women To Watch" series. Mayer has been a featured speaker on many panels in the Philadelphia area and has guest lectured at a number of Universities, where her talks focus on how emerging artists can promote their work and sustain a career in the arts. A graduate of Bucknell University, Mayer was an active member of the University's Arts Board for several years.

ABOUT BRIDGETTE MAYER BUSINESSES

Bridgette Mayer Gallery exhibits, represents, and promotes artists from around the world through our established gallery program in Philadelphia, as well as our art advisory firm based in the greater Los Angeles area.

Building on 15 years of experience in the international art market, our professionally curated program facilitates access to innovative works from a diverse group of artists engaged on both a local and global scale. Bridgette Mayer Gallery is a leader in the Philadelphia arts community, actively partnering with local organizations to support fundraising initiatives and generate opportunities for our artists to engage with the public. For more information: www.bridgettemayergallery.com or www.bridgettemayerartadvisors.com.

Made in United States
Orlando, FL
19 November 2021

10528210R00107